THE COMPLETE WORKS OF
LAO TZU

THE COMPLETE WORKS OF
LAO TZU

TAO TEH CHING
AND
HUA HU CHING

An Enlightening New
Translation and Elucidation
by
Hua Ching Ni

TAO OF
WELLNESS

Los Angeles

We wish to thank the Bildarchiv Foto Marburg in Marburg,West Germany for the use of the artwork on the cover and all the students and friends who assisted with the publication of this book.

All of the Chinese calligraphy in this book was written by Hua-Ching Ni.

Tao of Wellness
13315 Washington Boulevard Suite 200
Los Angeles, CA 90066
www.taoofwellness.com

The material in this book is more than a translation, it is an elucidation drawing upon Hua-Ching Ni's decades of spiritual cultivation and training in the tradition in which these works originated. Anyone who wishes to produce their own version of this material should work directly from an original text rather than copying from Hua-Ching Ni's work.

The paper used in this publication meets the minimum requirements of the American National Standard for Information Sciences Permanence of Paper for Printed Library Materials, ANSI 239.48- 1984.

First Printing July 1979   Seventh Printing April 1993
Second Printing June 1980   Eighth Printing June 1995
Third Printing May 1982   Ninth Printing January 1997
Fourth Printing October 1986   Tenth Printing October 1998
Fifth Printing February 1989   Eleventh Printing June 2000
Sixth Printing March 1991   Twelfth Printing February 2003
Thirteenth Printing Sept 2006   Fourteenth printing Sept 2008

Library of Congress Cataloging-in-Publication Data
Lao-tzu.
    [Tao te ching. English]
    The complete works of Lao Tzu : Tao the ching and Hua
hu ching / translation and elucidation by Hua-Ching.
    p. cm.
    Includes index.
    ISBN 10: 0-937064-00-9 (alk.paper)
    ISBN 13: 978-0937064009 $15.95
    I. Ni, Hua Ching. II. Lao-tzu. Hua hu ching. English. 1993.
III. Title.
BL1900.L26E5 1993f   93-40285
299'.51482-dc20   CIP

*This book is dedicated to
those who cherish a broad spiritual attitude
and appreciate the wisdom of natural inspiration
in giving the light of perpetual value
to guide all people of all generations.*

To all readers,

According to the teaching of the Universal Integral Way, male and female are equally important in the natural sphere. This fact is confirmed in the diagram of *T'ai Chi*. Thus, discrimination is not practiced in our tradition. All of my work is dedicated to both genders of the human race.

Wherever possible, constructions using masculine pronouns to represent both sexes are avoided. Where they occur, we ask your tolerance and spiritual understanding. We hope that you will take the essence of my teaching and overlook the limitations of language. Gender discrimination is inherent in English. Ancient Chinese pronouns do not differentiate gender. I wish that all of you will achieve yourselves well above the level of language and gender. Thank you.

Warning - Disclaimer

This book is intended to present information and techniques that have been in use throughout the Orient for many years. This information and these practices utilize a natural system within the body; however, no claims are made regarding their effectiveness. The information offered is according to the author's best knowledge and experience and is to be used by the reader at his or her own discretion and liability.

Because of the sophisticated nature of the information contained within this book, it is recommended that the reader also study the author's other books for a broader understanding of energy-conducting exercises and a healthy lifestyle.

People's lives have different conditions and their growth has different stages. Because the background of people's development cannot be unified, there is no single practice that can be universally applied to everyone. Thus, it must be through the discernment of the reader that the practices are selected. The adoption and application of the material offered in this book must therefore be the reader's own responsibility.

The author and publisher of this book are not responsible in any manner for any harm that may occur through following the instructions in this book.

THE UNIVERSAL WAY

*The Universal Way is the destination
        of all spiritual efforts of humankind.
It serves all people's lives,
        everywhere and always.*

*The Universal Way conveys the deep truth
        of all conscious elaborations of the human mind.
It contains the vast and profound essence
        of the human spirit.
Thus it transcends all religious teachings,
        leaving them behind,
        like the clothing of a bygone season.*

*The Universal Way is the goal of all sciences,
        but is not locked at the level of the intellect.
It cuts through all wasteful skepticism
        and inexhaustible searching.
Thus it surpasses all sciences,
        leaving them behind
        like historical relics of the past.*

*The Subtle Essence that is sought
        by all sciences and all religions
        transcends all attempts to reach it
        by means of thought, belief or experiment.
The Universal Way leads directly to it
        and guides you to reach it yourself
        by uniting with the Integral Nature of the Universe.*

*The Universal Way is like the master key
        to all doors leading to the inner room
        of ultimate truth.
It is the master teaching of all teachings,
        yet it relies on no religions and no experiments.
There is no need for intellectual or emotional detours
        that cannot serve the lives of all people
        everywhere and always.
Follow the Universal Way beyond all boundaries
        to the heart and essence of natural life itself.*

道德經

Tao Teh Ching

INTRODUCTION TO
TAO TEH CHING

Lao Tzu's *Tao Teh Ching* is one of the most cherished and frequently translated works in the world. Its pages contain the simple yet most profound truths of the universe. Among ancient achieved people, Lao Tzu is considered the greatest teacher of all time and his given spiritual title is "Most Exalted One." He is regarded as a sage of highly revered energy, and legend states that he spent eighty-one years in his mother's womb. In plain language, this means that it took many years for him to bear the fruit of wisdom.

As keeper of the ancient archives, Lao Tzu was well-versed in the wisdom and knowledge of China's greatest sages before the time of the Yellow Emperor (2697 B.C.E.). His official position in the government was historiographer. In ancient culture, the historiographer was also in charge of observing celestial phenomena and consulting the *I Ching* for the imperial court. This custom continued throughout ancient times until the end of the Chou Dynasty.

As time passed, Lao Tzu became aware that a time of great confusion and spiritual disintegration was about to befall the empire. He decided to leave society and live a life in harmony with nature. Thus he rode westward on the back of a water buffalo. When he came to the Han Gu pass at the border of China, he was requested by the pass official to write down the essence of his wisdom. This classic has since been called the *Tao Teh Ching. Tao* means the integral truth of the universe, *Teh* means the virtuous application of such high, subtle knowledge, and *Ching* means serious spiritual guidance.

Lao Tzu's official duty as *I Ching* consultant for the

state took him deeply into and beyond the *I Ching*. The *I Ching* was derived from simple ancient mathematics, but the ancients extended their minds beyond numbers. When the mind is fresh, it is easy to receive inspiration. The basic question is, why there are odd and even numbers? If you give up this basic structure of odd and even, no mathematics can possibly go further and no result can be inferred. By answering this simple question, you find the basic frame of *yin* and *yang,* the basic pattern of the intellectual mind. Most people know some mathematics, but few ever question why there are odd and even numbers. The simple fact is similar to an apple falling from a tree, which kindled the discovery of Isaac Newton.

All cultural inspiration starts very simply, but after editing and reediting, the original simplicity is lost. It is the same once a great conception, philosophy or system of thought is turned into a religion, the original thought dies off. This is why I have such a deep appreciation for the Way: because its attitudes stay open to development, correction, improvement and refinement without insisting upon a final truth. The ultimate truth is beyond definition, although we all attempt to define it. All religions harm the original spirit of life by condemning natural things as sex and eating as sins, never noticing they hold the power to continue human life. Rejecting something that is essential to life is human foolishness. This is why the sages said, "Let us just be quiet and let the world's people fool around for another million years."

The teachings of Lao Tzu are both rational and miraculous. They appear to be like a cup of clear, flavorless water, yet their subtle profundity is immeasurable. They are an expression of utmost simplicity and purest wisdom. They enable people at all levels of development to partake of this wisdom, just as pure water refreshes and supports all aspects of life. Many, however, are unable to accept this subtle power and mystical vision because these unadorned teachings do not arouse their imagination or stimulate their illusions. If these teachings did this, however, they would only be another impediment to true inner growth.

The truth is to keep moving. If you get stuck in one concept, the truth dies. This is why I call this teaching the Integral Truth.

T.A.O.
Truth **A**bove **O**neself
Truth **A**mong **O**urselves

Tao is the Integral Truth of the Universe
Teh is the application of the universal truth.
Ching is holy book or route.

道無為　無不為　可心證
非智知　何謂知　何謂證
知道智　證虛應　應無從
心乃通　通於一　萬事畢
一為根　事為門　事歸一
一常存　存莫有　假言守
守虛無　自長久

右大道守一寶章

己未清和

ONE

Tao, the subtle reality of the universe
cannot be described.
That which can be described in words
is merely a conception of the mind.
Although names and descriptions have been applied to it,
the subtle reality is beyond the description.

One may use the word "Nothingness"
to describe the Origin of the universe,
and "Beingness"
to describe the Mother of the myriad things,
but Nothingness and Beingness are merely conceptions.

From the perspective of Nothingness,
one may perceive the expansion of the universe.
From the perspective of Beingness,
one may distinguish individual things.
Both are for the conceptual convenience of the mind.

Although different concepts can be applied,
Nothingness and Beingness
and other conceptual activity of the mind
all come from the same indescribable subtle Originalness.
The Way is the unfoldment of such subtle reality.
Having reached the subtlety of the universe,
one may see the ultimate subtlety,
the Gate of All Wonders.

TWO

*A*s soon as the world regards something
    as beautiful,
  ugliness simultaneously becomes apparent.
 As soon as the world regards something as good,
    evil simultaneously becomes apparent.

In exactly the same manner,
    existence and nonexistence give birth to each other.
 Difficult and easy define each other.
 Long and short form each other.
 High and low make each other distinguishable.
 Silence and sound make each other conspicuous.
 Front and back connect each other.

Realizing this, one does not separate one's being
    from the subtle essence of the universe.
 One holds no preconceptions, and does things
    without insisting on personal conditions.
 One guides people by living in accord
    with the essence of life.
 One brings good things about,
    but has no intention of possessing them.
 One performs work,
    but has no intention to acquire personal power.

When one's task is accomplished,
  one lets go of it and seeks no reward or recognition.
Because one does not claim credit for oneself,
  one does not do any damage to oneself.

THREE

When the superior are not exalted,
*   envy will not be aroused.*
Then there will be no rivalry or contention among people.
When wealth is not treasured,
*   desire for possessions will not be stirred up.*
Then people will not be tempted to rob one another.
By shutting that which is desirable out of sight,
*   the heart will remain undisturbed.*
Then there will be no confusion in the hearts of people.

The guidance of the Universal One
*   of natural wholeness is therefore:*
Empty your mind.
Enjoy good health.
Weaken your ambitions.
Strengthen your essence.

When people are free from cunning, desire, and artifice,
*   everything will be well-ordered of its own accord.*

FOUR

The subtle Way of the universe
appears to lack strength,
yet its power is inexhaustible.
Fathomless, it could be the origin of all things.
It has no sharpness,
yet it rounds off all sharp edges.
It has no form,
yet it unties all tangles.
It has no glare,
yet it merges all lights.
It harmonizes all things
and unites them as one integral whole.
It seems so obscure,
yet it is the Ultimate Clarity.
Whose offspring it is can never be known.
It is that which existed before any divinity.

FIVE

The subtle virtue of the universe is wholeness.
It regards all things as equal.
The virtue of the sage is wholeness.
He too regards all things as equal.

The universe may be compared to a bellows.
It is empty,
*   yet it never fails to generate its products.*
The more it moves,
*   the more it brings forth.*

Many words lead one nowhere.
Many pursuits in different directions
*   bring only exhaustion.*
Rather, embrace the subtle essence within.

SIX

*T*he subtle essence of the universe is active.
    It is like an unfailing fountain of life
    which flows forever in a vast and profound valley.
It is called the Primal Female and the Subtle Origin.
The Gate of the Subtle Origin
    becomes the root of the universe.
It subtly and gently generates
    without exhausting itself.

SEVEN

Heaven is everlasting and Earth is perpetual.
    Why so? Because they live
    without holding onto any consciousness of self.
Therefore, they can endure forever.
One who does not separate his being
    from the nature of universal wholeness
    lives with the universal virtue of wholeness.
He, too, dissolves all consciousness of self
    and lives as the universe.
By putting himself behind others,
    he finds himself foremost.
By not considering his own personal ends,
    his personal life is accomplished.
He finds himself safe, secure and preserved.
Because he does not hold a narrow concept of self,
    his true nature can fully merge
    with the one universal life.

EIGHT

*O*ne *of universal nature is like water;*
    he benefits all things
  but does not contend with them.
He unprotestingly takes the lowest position;
  thus, he is close to the universal truth.

One of universal virtue chooses to live
  in a suitable environment.
He attunes his mind to become profound.
He deals with others with kindness.
In his speech, he is sincere.
His rule brings about order.
His work is efficient.
His actions are opportune.

One of deep virtue does not contend with people;
  thus, he is above reproach.

NINE

A bow that is stretched to its fullest capacity
   may certainly snap.
A sword that is tempered to its very sharpest
   may easily be broken.
A house that is full of jade and gold
   cannot remain secure for long.
One who proudly displays his wealth invites trouble.
Therefore, resign from a high position
   when your mission is complete.
This is the Universal Way of a life of deep virtue.

TEN

Can you always embrace Oneness
     without the slightest separation of body and mind?
Can you maintain undivided concentration
     until your vital force is as supple as a newborn baby's?
Can you clarify your inner vision to be flawless?
Can you love your people and serve your state
     with no self-exaltation?
As Life's Gate opens and closes
     in the performance of birth and death,
     can you maintain the receptive, feminine principle
     when yin and yang are changing?
After achieving the crystal clear mind,
     can you remain detached and innocent?

Give birth to and nourish all things
     without desiring to possess them.
Give of yourself,
     without expecting something in return.
Assist people, but do not attempt to control them.
This is how to realize the deep virtue of the universe.

ELEVEN

Thirty spokes together make a wheel for a cart.
It is the empty space in the center
which enables it to be used.
Mold clay into a vessel;
it is the emptiness within
that creates the usefulness of the vessel.
Cut out doors and windows in a house;
it is the empty space inside
that creates the usefulness of the house.
Thus, what we have may be something substantial,
But its usefulness lies in the unoccupied, empty space.
The substance of your body is enlivened
by maintaining the part of you that is unoccupied.

TWELVE

*T*he five basic colors
   can be made into countless combinations
   to perplex the eyes.
The five basic tones
   can be made into infinite compositions
   to bewilder the ears.
The five basic flavors
   can be made into numerous stimulations
   to confuse the tongue.
The pursuit of worldly pleasures
   can make the mind wild and uncontrollable.
The one who sees the deep nature of life
   would rather embrace
   the simple subtle essence of life.

THIRTEEN

*F*avor and disgrace are both causes of shock.
   When one is favored, one is shocked.
When one is disgraced, one is also shocked.
That is because people forget the unadorned plainness
   of universal life.
If they knew this clearly, then what is meant by saying
   that favor and disgrace are both causes of shock?
Favor is no higher than disgrace.

What is meant by saying that the greatest trouble
   is the strong sense of individual self
   that people carry in all circumstances?
People are beset with great trouble
   because they define their lives so narrowly.
If they forsake their narrow sense of self
   and live wholly, then what can they call trouble?

Therefore, only one who dedicates himself
   to the wholeness of the world is fit to tend the world.
Only one who relinquishes the self can be
   entrusted with responsibility for the life of the world.

FOURTEEN

*L*ook at it, but you cannot see it.
    Because it is formless, you call it invisible.
Listen to it, but you cannot hear it.
Because it is soundless, you call it inaudible.
Grasp it, but it is beyond your reach.
Because it is subtle, you call it intangible.
These three are indescribable and imperceptible,
    but in the mystical moment
    you see it, hear it and grasp it,
        the Unseen, Unheard and Unreachable
        presents itself as the indefinable essence.
Confront it, and you do not see its face.
Follow it, and you do not see its back.
It does not appear bright when viewed at the zenith.
Nor does it appear dark when viewed at the nadir.
There is nothing that can make this subtle essence
    of the universe distinct.
When you try to make it clear to yourself,
    it evasively reverts to Nothingness.

You may call it the Form of the Formless
    or the Image of the Imageless.
Yet the elusive, subtle essence remains nameless.
If you hope to meet it,
    it has no part you can call front.
If you hope to follow it,
    it has no place you can call behind.
Yet it can be observed
    in the constant regularity of the universe.
The constancy of the universe of antiquity
    is the constancy of the present time.

If one knows the Primal Beginning,
    one may thus know the truth
    of the universal subtle Way.

FIFTEEN

*The ancient ones who knew how to live
with the subtle essence of the universe
were gentle and flexible, profound and indistinguishable.
They were too deep to be known,
thus we can only describe their appearance.
They did not rush into anything,
as if fording an icy stream in early winter.
They were retiring and hesitant, not assertive,
as if they were shy of people.
They were reverent in demeanor to everyone,
as if meeting honored guests.
They did not insist on imposing their views on others
or interfering in worldly affairs,
as if they were passing travelers.*

*They adapted themselves to a circumstance
like melting ice.*

Simple and genuine, they were like virgin timber.
Empty and receptive, they were like a huge cave.
Comprehensive and unprejudiced,
  they were equally kind to all things;
  like the water of a stream flowing
  down a mountain, they benefitted all things.
Who else could move constantly
  from the gross and heavy to the light and pure?
Who else could evolve steadily
  from the inert and stagnant to everlasting life?

Those who hold fast to the subtle essence of the universe
  do not desire to extend themselves in climax.
Because there is no climax to one's extension and expansion,
  life is continually renewing itself.

SIXTEEN

*A*ttain the utmost unoccupiedness.
    Maintain the utmost stillness,
   and do not interfere with all the things
   that rush together in activity and grow luxuriantly.
Then you can see how living things flourish
   and renew themselves.
Yet, they all must return to the root again,
   each to its simple source.
Knowing to return to the root is to be refreshed.
This is called subtle revitalization.
To restore one's vitality is to constantly renew oneself.

To know constant renewal is to have achieved clarity.
If one does not know constant self renewal
   and thus acts foolishly,
   disaster will soon occur.
Knowing constancy in renewing oneself,
   one can extend the duration of one's life.
If one can deeply understand the extension of life's duration,
   one is able to contain all things within oneself.

To be all-inclusive is to be impartial.
To be impartial is to realize the positive,
    creative virtues of Heaven.
To be Heavenly is to be one with
    the subtle essence of the universe.
To be one with the subtle essence of the universe
    is to enjoy everlasting life.
Such a one will be preserved,
    even after the dissolution of his physical body.

SEVENTEEN

---

*H*igh beings of deep universal virtue
      work unassertively.
They help all people,
      yet people are barely aware of their existence.
Leaders of great achievement
      earn the friendship and praise of people.
Leaders of great strength make people afraid.
People despise and defy a leader
      who is untrustworthy.

One cannot inspire confidence in people
      through words alone;
      it must be accompanied by correct deeds.
When one of subtle virtue has accomplished his task,
      all the people will say:
      "It is we ourselves who made it so."

EIGHTEEN

When humankind strayed
from the natural way of life,
relative social disciplines began to appear.
When intelligence and cleverness of mind are admired,
great hypocrisy is born.
When disharmony manifested in family relations,
children who respected their parents
and parents who loved their children
became rare examples.
When chaos prevailed in the country,
only a few loyal ministers were recognized.

Let all people return to their true nature.
Love, kindness, wisdom, family harmony, and loyalty
should not be taught one by one,
separately from an honest life.
Then, once again,
people will regain the natural virtue of wholeness.
The world will be naturally ordered.
There will be no one who singly and cunningly
works for personal interest alone.

NINETEEN

*A*bandon the separate concepts
    of holiness and unholiness.
Then all people will be benefitted a hundredfold.
Abandon the separate concepts
    of justice and humanism,
    and all people will return
    to a natural state of harmony.
Abandon the cunning and cleverness of the mind,
    and people will cease to rob and deceive one another.
These things are based on artifice and are thus
    inadequate to express the natural virtue of wholeness.
Hence, return to the true self
    to embrace only the one, unadorned nature.
Refine personal preference and desire.
End the endless search
    for segmented, intellectual knowledge,
    and set your mind above worry and vexation.
In this way, one may restore one's unity
    with the perfection of one great universal life.

TWENTY

In high truth,
   is there any difference between yes and no?
Between good and evil,
   is there any absolute distinction?
Must one fear what everyone fears?
It is still too early for the subtle truth
   to dawn on those who are so self-assertive.

The people of the world run about excitedly as if they
   were going to miss the yearly, royal, sacrificial feast,
   or as if they were going to be the last one
   to climb a high tower on a beautiful spring day.
I alone remain quiet and indifferent.
I anchor my being to that which existed
   before Heaven and Earth were formed.
I alone am innocent and unknowing,
   like a newborn babe.
Unoccupied by worldly cares,
   I move forward to nowhere.

The people of the world have more than enough.
I alone appear to have nothing.
The people of the world appear shrewd and wise.
I alone look foolish.
I like to be forgotten by the world and left alone.

Indeed, I have the mind of a single person!
Calm and self-contained, I am like the vast ocean.
Free and seemingly aimless, I am like a gentle wind.

Everyone seems so clever and self-assured.
I alone appear unlearned and original,
    insistent upon a different direction
    than other people pursue.
I alone value taking my sustenance
    from the Mother.

TWENTY-ONE

One of deep virtue
    cherishes the subtle essence of the universe.
The subtle essence of the universe
    is elusive and evasive.
Though it is elusive and evasive,
    it unveils itself as images and forms.
Evasive and elusive,
    it discloses itself as indefinable substance.
Shadowy and indistinct,
    it reveals itself as impalpable subtle essence.
This essence is so subtle, and yet so real.
It is the subtle origin
    of the whole of creation and non-creation.
It existed prior to the beginning of time
    as the single deep and subtle reality of the universe.
It brings all into being.

TWENTY-TWO

*T**he yielding are preserved whole.*
  The crooked become straight.
The empty become filled.
The depleted are renewed.
What has little will gain.
What has much will become confused.

Therefore, one with a whole mind
  holds fast to the one essence
  and thereby becomes an example
  to the rest of the world.
Because he does not flaunt his brightness,
  he becomes enlightened.
Because he is not self-important,
  he becomes illustrious.
Because he does not boast of his accomplishments,
  he becomes successful.
Because he is not self-assertive, he becomes supreme.
Because he does not strive for superiority,
  there is no one in the world
  who can contend with his superiority.
Indeed, the ancient teaching that
  "the yielding are preserved whole" is no empty saying.
Truly, they are preserved whole
  in order to attain one universal life.

TWENTY-THREE

The utterance of the universal subtle law
     is too loud to be audible.
Look at this:
     a squall does not last the whole morning,
     nor does a torrential shower last the whole day.
What determines this?
Even Nature cannot make such violence *last for long.*
How long, then, can the violent actions
     of human beings last?

Hence, one who follows gentleness
     becomes one with universal truth.
One who follows wholeness
     becomes one with universal virtue.
One who separates himself from universal nature
     and from universal virtue
     becomes separate and lost.

When one is one with universal nature,
     universal nature is one with him.
When one is one with universal virtue,
     universal virtue is one with him.
When one deviates from universal nature,
     deviation keeps him from universal nature.
If one does not know and believe that the subtle law
     manifests in his own life,
     how can he have faith
     that it pervades the entire universe?

TWENTY-FOUR

*O*ne who stands on tiptoe cannot stand firmly.
   One who strides cannot walk far.
One who flaunts himself is not illumined.
One who insists that he is right is self-righteous.
One who boasts of his accomplishments undoes his merit.
One who takes pride in himself impedes his own growth.

These things are normally detested by
   people who nurture virtue and the truthfulness of life,
   for they do not set their eyes and hearts
   upon anything that is equal to
   "the greed for excessive food
   which fosters morbid growth."
Thus, such things are not agreeable to them.

TWENTY-FIVE

Before Heaven and Earth are born,
        there is something formless
    and complete in itself.
Impalpable and everlasting,
        silent and undisturbed,
        standing alone and unchanging,
        it exercises itself gently,
        and generates itself inexhaustively
        in all dimensions.
It may be regarded as the Mother of all things.
Far beyond humankind's relative conception,
        it cannot be referred to by a specific name,
        yet it may be identified
        as the subtle essence of the universe.
In the absence of an accurate word,
        I shall call it "the Great."
Being great, it extends itself without limit.
Extending itself without limit, it is far-reaching.
Being far-reaching, it ultimately reverts to itself,
        returning to its self-sufficient origin.
Indeed, it had never really left itself!
This indefinable subtle energy flow
        is truly the greatest of all.

Expressing its integral nature,
        the universal subtle essence remains intangible,
        yielding, and uncontrollable:
        the ultimate expression of the cosmos.

As an expression of its unceasing creativeness,
    it manifests as the spaciousness of the sky.
As an expression of its receptiveness,
    it manifests as the great massiveness
    of galaxies, stars, and planets.
As an expression of harmonious reintegration,
    it manifests as human life.

Thus, in the natural flow of energy transformation,
    human life becomes one of the four great expressions
    of the subtle essence of the universe.
It is the way of universal subtle integration.
Humankind conforms to Earth.
Earth conforms to the sky.
The sky conforms to the Subtle Origin.
The Subtle Origin conforms to its own nature.

These are the four peaks of manifestation
    from the great transformation
    of one universal subtle energy.
Taking an individual human life as example,
    the intangible body with its fluids and nervous system
    construct a field of intangible,
    but functioning mind and super consciousness.

TWENTY-SIX

C *enteredness is the cure for impulsiveness.*
     Serenity is the master of restlessness.
Knowing this, one of universal nature is placid
    and never departs from the center of his own being.
Though he may move about all day,
    he never loses his poise.
Though he may be surrounded by splendor and comfort,
    he is always dispassionate and undistracted.
For one with great responsibility,
    to conduct himself lightly is perilous.
In frivolity, one's root is lost.
In restlessness, one's self-mastery could go with the wind!

TWENTY-SEVEN

*O ne who is good at running leaves no tracks.
One who is good at talking
has no flaws in his speech.
One who is good at calculating
makes no use of counting tools.
One who is good at shutting things
makes no use of bolt and bar
yet no one can open what he has shut.
One who is good at tying
makes no use of cords and knots,
yet no one can untie what he has fastened.
One of natural, integral virtue
is good at helping all people impartially.
Thus, no one is abandoned.
Because he is good at protecting and preserving all things,
nothing is ever thrown away.
This is called "embodying the light of the subtle truth."*

*Hence, the people on the Universal Integral Way
are teachers of those off the Way.
However, if the student does not value the teacher,
and the teacher does not tend the student well,
though they both may be intelligent enough,
this leads only to further separation.*

TWENTY-EIGHT

*K*now *that you possess the strong masculine principle,*
yet abide by the meek, feminine principle.
Thus, become the flowing stream of the world.
As the flowing stream of the world,
never swerve from your true nature.
In this way, you return to the originality
of a newborn babe.

Know the bright, yet keep to the dark.
Never wavering from the subtle truth,
you will conform to the pattern of an integral being.
In this way, you return again to the infinite.

Know how to be honored and glorified,
yet maintain unadorned plainness.
Thus, become the abundant valley of the world.
As the abundant valley of the world,
you realize the sufficiency of the constant,
subtle virtue of the integral universe.
In this way, you return to the original simplicity
of an uncarved block of wood
with undamaged potential.

An integral individual,
      by preserving the original qualities of his being,
      maintains his supreme, integral nature.
When the uncarved block is shaped
      into various single tools and vessels,
      its original qualities are destroyed.
This is called
      "the great Oneness that cannot be divided."

TWENTY-NINE

*T*hose who want to conquer the world
   and make it conform to their own desires
  will never have success,
   for the sovereignty of the world is a subtle thing.
He who tries to shape it spoils it.
He who tries to hold it loses it.

The things of the world are constantly changing.
There is a time for things to move ahead,
   and a following time for things to retreat;
  a time to withdraw internally,
   and a following time to expand externally;
  a time to grow luxuriantly,
   and a following time to decay;
  a time to rise up,
   and a following time to sink down low.

Therefore, one who does not separate his being
   from the deep nature of the universe
  avoids all extremes, extravagance and excess.

THIRTY

*O*ne who assists a leader with the subtle truth
     of the universe advises him
  not to use the force of arms
  to try to conquer the world,
  for such things will always rebound.
It is generally the nature of weapons
  to turn against their wielders.

Whenever armies touch the land,
  they turn it into a wasteland.
Moreover, plague and death invariably follow
  in the wake of a great war.

Therefore, a leader should be allowed
  to effect only a right purpose
  and not rely on the force of arms
  once his goal has been achieved.
He effects his right purpose,
  but does not take pride in it.
He effects his right purpose
  as a regrettable necessity.
He effects his right purpose,
  but does not delight in violence,
  for he knows that to be excessively strong
  is to hasten decay and that violence
  is against the integral nature of the universe.
Whoever goes against the nature of the universe
  will soon perish.

THIRTY-ONE

*W*eapons are instruments of killing
    and destruction,
  which are contrary to the nature of life.
Thus, they are avoided by those who follow
  the subtle Way of the universe.

According to ancient social custom,
    in times of peace a gentleman regards the left side,
    the soft hand, as the place of honor;
    in times of war, the right side, the strong hand,
    is considered the place of honor.

Because weapons are inauspicious,
    they are not the instruments of a gentleman.
Only when one has no other choice
    may one resort to using them,
    and, if their use is necessary,
    one must employ calmness and restraint,
    for peace and quiet are the normal nature
    of universal life.

Even in victory there is no cause
    for excitement and rejoicing.
To rejoice over a victory
    is to delight in killing and destruction.
He who delights in killing and destruction
    cannot be expected to thrive for long in the world.

Therefore, on happy occasions
the left side has precedence,
while on sad occasions, it is the right side.

When this rite was applied in the army,
the lieutenant-commander stood at the left,
while the commander-in-chief stood on the right.
This indicates that war is treated
as the equivalent of a funeral service.
Because many people
have been caused an unnatural death in war,
it is only right that the survivors should mourn them.
Even when a victory is won,
the occasion should be regarded as lamentable.

THIRTY-TWO

*T*he universal subtle essence is unnameable
    and omnipresent.
Although it appears even in the plainest
    and most ordinary of things,
    it is inferior to nothing.
It maintains itself as a model of indivisible integrity.
If people would embrace it as their own true nature,
    everything would settle down
    in right order and peace of its own accord.
Harmonious relationship can be illustrated
    by the cycle of the seasons
    which produces rain and dew
    at exactly the right times.
People do not need to do anything
    to insure the harmony between Heaven and Earth.

All names were given for the purpose of distinction
    when the original simplicity was diversified.
When one departs from simplicity, the result is perplexity.
When one returns to simplicity,
    one is saved from destruction by confusion.

The universal subtle essence is to human beings
    what the great ocean is to the rivers
    and streams of the earth.

THIRTY-THREE

---

*O*ne who knows others is clever.
       One who knows himself has insight.
One who overcomes others is forceful.
One who overcomes himself is truly strong.
One who knows he has enough is rich.
One who does not divert his mind from
       the realization of integral virtue is wisely willful.
One who preserves his natural integrity will endure.
One who embraces the subtle essence dies
       yet does not perish
       and thus enjoys true immortality.

THIRTY-FOUR

The subtle essence of the universe
    is omnipresent.
It may go to the left or the right.
All things derive their life from it,
    and it holds nothing back from them,
    yet it takes possession of nothing.
It accomplishes its purpose,
    but it claims no merit.
It clothes and feeds all,
    but has no ambition to be master over anyone.
Thus it may be regarded as "the Small."
All things return to it, and it contains them,
    yet it claims no authority over them.
Thus it may be recognized as "the Great."
The wise one who never attempts
    to be emotionally great
    and who accomplishes each small task with full devotion,
    as if it were the greatest of tasks,
    is naturally recognized as great.

THIRTY-FIVE

When the subtle Way of the universe is taught,
*   people know where to go and what to learn,*
because they know that they will not be harmed
but will receive great peace.
The teacher of the universal Way
*   is like one who gives real food to people.*
He does not feed them colorful bait
*   with the intention of catching them.*

The subtle Way of the universe is flavorless,
*   with nothing much to offer the mouth.*
Neither does it offer much
*   to be enjoyed by the eyes or entertain the ears,*
*   yet its usefulness is inexhaustible.*

THIRTY-SIX

If you hope to expand,
*   you should first contract.*
If you hope to become strong,
*   you should first weaken yourself.*
If your ambition is to be exalted,
*   humiliation will follow.*
If you hold fast to something,
*   it will surely be taken away from you.*
This is the operation of the subtle law of the universe.

The law of the universe is subtle,
*   but it can be known.*
The soft and meek can overcome the hard and strong.
The strength of a country must not be displayed.
Just as fish cannot leave the deep,
*   one must never stray from one's true nature.*

THIRTY-SEVEN

The subtle essence of the universe
is always unoccupied,
  yet it leaves nothing undone.
If the people of the world were wise enough
  to plant the root of their lives
  deep within the Subtle Origin,
  then the worldly affairs of life
  would coherently follow their own natural course,
  and harmony would abound of its own accord.
When confusion takes place in one's surroundings,
  it can be dissolved with the power
  of undisturbable Simplicity.
When life is ruled by undisturbable Simplicity,
  desire and passion naturally fall away
  and reveal people's true, original nature.
Then the peaceful order of the universe prevails
  and unity manifests again of its own accord.

THIRTY-EIGHT

O *ne of subtle universal virtue*
*   is not conscious of being virtuous,*
*   therefore, he is truly virtuous.*
One of partial virtue attempts to live up to
*   an external standard of virtue.*
Therefore, he is not truly virtuous.
One of whole virtue does not need to do anything
*   in order to be virtuous,*
*   because virtue is the very essence*
*   of one's true nature.*
But, one of partial virtue believes that something
*   must be done in order to prove that he is virtuous.*
Thus, partial virtue becomes prevalent
*   when people fail to follow their own true nature.*
Benevolence becomes prevalent
*   when people fail to be naturally kind.*
Etiquette becomes prevalent
*   when people fail to be righteous and considerate.*
When people find no response with etiquette,
*   they roll up their sleeves*
*   and force others to respond to them.*

When people stray from the subtle way of universal nature,
they can no longer perceive their own true nature.
Thus, they emphasize relative virtue.
When natural virtue is lost,
society depends on the doctrine of humanism.
When humanity becomes corrupted,
social and religious teachings appear
and become powerful forces.
When social and religious teachings become corrupted,
what is left behind is the empty shell
of superficial ceremonies and artificial etiquette.
When etiquette is emphasized,
it is because people lack the simple qualities
of fairness and kindness.
This is the starting point of people of confusion.
All of these man-made, partial virtues
are merely superficial flowers, a false nature.
When people begin to move away
from their own true nature,
it is the beginning of hypocrisy.

Therefore, one who integrates
  his own individual being
  with the deep nature of the universe
  sets his heart upon the root of reality
  rather than the husk,
  and upon the nourishment of the fruit
  rather than the fleeting beauty of the flowers.

Truly, he cherishes what is deep within
  rather than what is shallow without.
Knowing this,
  he knows what to accept and what to reject.

THIRTY-NINE

*S*ince ancient times there have been those
who have attained the subtle essence of the universe
and thus become what they are.
Heaven attained the subtle essence of the universe
and became clear.
Earth attained the subtle essence of the universe
and became stable.
Divine spirits attained the subtle essence of the universe
and became powerful.
The Valley of the Universe attained
the subtle essence of the universe
and became productive.
The myriad things attained the subtle essence
of the universe and became prosperous.
The sages attained the subtle essence
of the universe and became wise
All became what they are
by attaining the subtle essence of the universe
and hence their true nature.

Extinction happens to one who violates his true nature.
Without being pure, Heaven would cease to be.
Without being stable, Earth would burst into bits.
Without maintaining their potency, spirits would disperse.
Without being productive,
    the vast Valley of the Universe
    would become exhausted.
Without being reproductive,
    the myriad things would perish.
Without fortifying themselves with integral virtue,
    sages would stumble and fall.

Greatness is rooted in plainness,
    just as the low forms the foundation of the high.
Realizing this, the ancient sovereigns
    were content to style themselves as
    desolate, unworthy, and needy.
Therefore, one who does not separate his being from
    the nature of the universe follows the Integral Way.
He has no wish to sound like jingling jade pendants
    in order to court a good name,
    nor like the rumbling of a stone rolling from a cliff
    in order to create a bad name.
Each one should work
    on one's own subtle spiritual integration
    with the subtle essence of the universe.

FORTY

*R*eturning to itself
  is how the subtle Way of the universe exercises itself.
Being gentle and yielding
  is how the subtle Way of the universe employs itself.
All things of the world come from the Manifest.
The Manifest comes from the unmanifest, subtle
  essence of the universe.

FORTY-ONE

*When people of the highest awareness
    hear the subtle Way of the universe,
they cultivate themselves diligently
in order to live in accord with it.
When mediocre people
    hear the subtle Way of the universe,
    they are unimpressed.
When people who are low
    hear the subtle Way of the universe,
    they break into loud laughter.
If it were not laughed at,
    it would not be the subtle Way of the universe.*

*Thus there is a traditional saying that
    he who understands the subtle Way of the universe
    seems dull of comprehension.
He who approaches the subtle Way of the universe
    seems to move away from it.
He who moves on the smooth path of the universe
    seems to go up and down as if traveling a rough road.
The deeply virtuous
    are like an empty, receptive valley.
The innocent appear to be sullied.
The abundant appear to be deficient.
The perfect appear to be defective.
The honest appear to be corrupt.*

Hence, great space has no corners.
Great talent ripens late.
Great eloquence is silent.
Great form is shapeless.

The subtle essence of the universe
  is hidden and indefinable,
  yet its benefit is always subtly bestowed.

FORTY-TWO

The universal subtle essence gave birth to One.
   One gave birth to Two.
Two gave birth to Three.
Three gave birth to the Myriad Things.
All lives have their backs to the yin and embrace the yang.

There is nothing more loathed by people
   than to be orphaned, desolate, and hapless.
Yet the wise ancient kings, princes, and barons
   used such titles to refer to themselves.
A thing is sometimes benefitted by being humbled,
   and diminished by being expanded.
What the ancients have taught, I also shall teach:
   "A man of force and violence
   will come to a violent end."
Whoever said this can be my teacher and father.

FORTY-THREE

*T*he softest of all things
    can overcome the hardest of all things.
Only the insubstantial can penetrate the spaceless.
Thus, we know the benefit of non-interference
    and the teaching of the subtle Way of the universe
    that does not rely on words.
Few people under Heaven can attain it.

FORTY-FOUR

As for your fame and your life,
*   which matters more?*
As for your life and your wealth,
*   which is more precious?*
As for gain or loss, which is more damaging?
He who is most endeared to something
*   must pay dearest for it.*
He who has hoarded much
*   will suffer great loss.*
He who knows when enough is enough
*   saves himself from humiliation.*
He who knows when to stop
*   protects himself from peril.*
To know this is to be long enduring.

FORTY-FIVE

*T*he great perfection seems imperfect,
    yet its usefulness is unfailing.
The great fullness appears to be void,
    yet its usefulness is boundless.
The great accomplishment seems unfinished.
The ultimate straightness appears crooked.
Profound skillfulness appears clumsy.
Fluent eloquence seems mute.

Movement overcomes cold.
Stillness overcomes heat.
Maintain clarity and purity,
    and be a model of deep virtue for all people.

FORTY-SIX

When the people of the world
live in accord with the subtle Way of the universe,
horses are used for agricultural purposes.
When the people of the world
do not live in accord with the subtle Way of the universe,
then horses, even pregnant mares,
are driven into the battlefield and bred there.
There is no greater calamity for a nation,
or for an individual,
than not finding contentment
with one's own sufficiency.
There is no greater mistake for a nation,
or for an individual, than to be covetous.
Hence, when one is content within one's own nature,
one will always have enough.

FORTY-SEVEN

*Without going out of your door,
    you can know the ways of the world.
Without looking through your window,
    you can see the Way of Heaven.
The farther you go, the less you know.
Thus, one of deep virtue knows without going,
    sees without looking,
    and accomplishes without doing.*

FORTY-EIGHT

*L*earning builds daily accumulation,
  but the practice of the Way of spiritual integration
  with the subtle essence of the universe
  builds daily simplification.
Simplify and simplify, until all contamination
  from relative, contradictory thinking is eliminated.
Then one does nothing, yet nothing is left undone.
One who wins the world
  does so by not meddling with it.
One who meddles with the world loses it.

FORTY-NINE

*O*ne with wholeness of virtue
  has an unconditioned mind.
He regards the mind of all being
   as his own mind.
He is kind to the kind.
He is also kind to the unkind,
   for the subtle nature of the universe is kind.
He is faithful to the faithful.
He is also faithful to the unfaithful,
   for the integral virtue of the universe is undeceiving.

In the midst of the world,
   he dissolves all minds into harmonious Oneness.
All people strain their eyes and ears for excitement.
One of deep virtue brings all people back
   to their childlike-heartedness.

FIFTY

*T*hat one's physical life will
    begin with birth and end in death seems a surety.
Also, in an individual life, the special opportunities
    of life and death are very much equal.
When there is an opportunity for death,
    there is an opportunity for life also.
When there is an unusual opportunity for life,
    it pulls one's life closer to death.
Aside from such opportunities,
    there is the personal effort to maintain normalcy.
This is much more reliable than the special opportunities
    which place one's life on the verge of life and death.
People of awareness value normalcy
    and forsake seeking special opportunities which
    hold the promise of increasing the strength of living.
Such things are eventually
    only ways to speed up one's life.
One who can enjoy his natural life
    is content with the life of simple normalcy.

As I was told, one who knows
   how to tend his life with simple normalcy,
   does not meet wild animals on the road
   or know the touch of weapons during war.
The mighty horns of the rhinoceros,
   the powerful claws of the tiger,
   the sharp blades of weapons,
   find nowhere to pierce him.
Why is this so?
Because his mind holds no uncanny thoughts
   he gives death no opportunity.

FIFTY-ONE

The natural essence of the universe
    gives life to all things.
Virtue nurses them.
Matter shapes them.
The natural environment brings them to maturity.
Therefore, all things without exception
    revere the subtle essence and honor virtue.
Though the subtle essence deserves reverence,
    it does not demand it.
And though virtue ought to be honored,
    it, too, does not demand it.

Thus, it is the subtle essence
    that gives life to all things,
    and with its virtue nurses them, grows them,
    fosters them, shelters them, comforts them,
    nourishes them and embraces them.

It does all this, yet it claims no possession,
    expects no gratitude, and desires no lordship.
This is called the subtle virtue of the universe.

FIFTY-TWO

All of creation has a common beginning.
This common beginning
is the Mysterious Mother of all.
If we know the Mother, we may know her offspring.
Know the offspring, yet stay with the Mother,
and the essence of your life will never be exhausted,
even though your body be dissolved.

Block the openings, shut the doors,
and to the end of your days, you will not be worn out.
Unblock the openings, multiply your activities,
and to the end of your days,
you will be beyond remedy.

Thus it is said:
To perceive the subtle is to have true vision.
To be soft is to be truly strong.
Use the outer light, but return to the inner.
In this way, you will restore your integral virtue,
and be preserved from all harm.

FIFTY-THREE

If I had even the tiniest grain of insight,
I should live in accordance with
the subtle Way of the universe;
my only fear would be to stray from it.
The Integral Way of the universe
is very smooth and straight,
yet people's minds prefer devious bypaths.

The courts are polished and decorated,
while the fields are untilled,
and the granaries are empty.
People wear fine clothes
to adorn their external appearance.
They carry sharp swords at their sides
and worship might rather than righteousness.
They know only to make merry
by indulging in food and drink.
They crave to possess more riches
than they could ever use.

This is the committing of robbery
and is not the Universal Integral Way of natural life.

FIFTY-FOUR

*W*hat is well planted cannot be pulled up.
*   What is closely embraced cannot slip away.*
The wise establish virtue firmly within themselves,
*   and are honored for generations ever after.*

Apply natural, integral virtue to your own character,
*   and it will be genuine.*
Apply natural, integral virtue to the family,
*   and it will abound.*
Apply natural, integral virtue to the state,
*   and it will flourish abundantly.*
Apply natural, integral virtue to the world,
*   and it will be pervasive.*

Understand other people's lives
*   by means of your own life.*
Understand other people's families
*   by means of your own family.*
Understand other societies
*   by means of your own society.*
Understand other countries
*   by means of your own country.*
How can you know what is right for the world?
By knowing what is right for your own life.

FIFTY-FIVE

*O*ne who is steeped in natural virtue
    is akin to a newborn babe.
Wasps and poisonous serpents do not sting it.
Fierce beasts do not seize it.
Birds of prey do not maul it.
Its bones are tender, its muscles soft, yet its grip is firm.
It has not known the union of male and female,
    yet its male member will stir naturally.
This is because its vitality is perfectly whole.
It can howl and scream all day long
    without becoming hoarse.
This is because it embodies perfect harmony.

To know harmony is to know natural virtue.
To recognize the natural virtue of the universe
    is to have insight.
To overprotect one's life is to invite danger.
To follow the fantasy of the mind
    is to drain away one's life energy.
To hasten growth is to hasten decay.
All of this is against the Way of natural virtue.
Whatever is against the Universal Way of life
    soon ceases to be.

FIFTY-SIX

*O*ne who knows does not speak.
   One who speaks does not know.
The one who knows is the one whose doors are shut,
   whose openings are blocked, whose sharpness
   is blunted, and whose glare is softened.
He is one with the subtle truth of the universe.

Thus you cannot get close to such a person
   by your love to do so.
Nor can you keep away from him
   by your desire to do so.
You cannot bestow benefit on him,
   nor can you do him harm,
   because he holds the subtle essence of the universe.

FIFTY-SEVEN

*W*hen serving the public, use upright means.
    When commanding troops in war,
   employ the principle of surprise.
To win the world, do nothing to interfere with it.
Why? Because the more prohibitions and inhibitions
   that are imposed on people,
   the more difficult their lives become.
The more destructive weapons a nation or its people
possess,
   the poorer the people of that country become,
   and the greater is the chaos that occurs in the world.
The more clever and crafty people become,
   the more often strange things happen.
The more laws and ordinances there are,
   the more criminals and dissidents will arise.

Therefore, the ancient sages of natural virtue said:
   "I do nothing, and people's contention
      dissolves by itself.
   I enjoy serenity, and people rectify themselves.
   I make no effort, and people enrich themselves.
   I have no desire, and people return to simplicity."

FIFTY-EIGHT

When the government does not interfere,
the people are simple and happy.
When the government does interfere,
the people are tense and cunning.
Disaster is what blessing perches on.
Blessing is where disaster abides.
Who can say what the ultimate end
of all possibilities will be?
Appropriate means soon become unfitting.
Good means soon turn to evil.
Long indeed have the people been perplexed
by the endless, topsy-turvy movement of life.
Therefore, one of subtle virtue
dissolves and eliminates the vicious cycle of duality.
He may have sharp corners, but he does not jab.
He may extend himself, but not at the expense of others.
He may shine, but he does not dazzle.

FIFTY-NINE

In managing people and serving Heaven,
*   there is nothing better*
*   than sparing unnecessary activities and expense.*
To be thrifty
*   means to return to the simple essence of life.*
To return to the simple essence of life
*   is to nourish subtle virtue.*
To nourish subtle virtue
*   is to be able to overcome any difficulty.*
Being able to overcome difficulties,
*   one can break through all limitations.*
One's limitlessness
*   is derived from whole and boundless virtue.*
The source of such virtue
*   can support one to serve a nation.*
Then one's benevolence can be enduring.
This is the way to firmly plant and deeply root oneself
*   in the subtle path of universal integration.*
This is the achievement of the Way of immortality.

SIXTY-FOUR

*T*ackle difficulties when they are easy.
    Accomplish great things when they are small.
Handle what is going to be rough
    when it is still smooth.
Control what has not yet formed its force.
Deal with a dangerous situation while it is safe.
Manage what is hard while it is soft.
Eliminate what is vicious
    before it becomes destructive.
This is called
    "attending to great things at small beginnings."

A tree so big it can fill the span of a man's arms
    grows from a tiny sprout.
A terrace nine stories high
    rises from a shovelful of earth.
A journey of a thousand miles
    begins with a single step.
Thus, one of integral virtue
    never sets about grandiose things,
    yet he is able to achieve great things.

Lightly made promises inspire little confidence.
Making light of things at the beginning,
    one will meet with failure in the end.
Being prepared for hardship,
one will not be overcome by it.
In handling their affairs, people often ruin them
    just as they are on the verge of success.
With heedfulness in the beginning
    and all the way through to the end,
    nothing is ruined.

SIXTY-FIVE

*I*n ancient times, those who were well-versed
     in the practice of the subtle Way of the universe
     did not lead people to disintegrate their minds
     through intellectual development for the sake of
     partial achievement.
Instead, they dissolved all contradictory concepts
     and images in order to maintain
     the natural state of simplicity.
Why are people so hard to manage?
Because they have become complicated.
He who leads others with a conditioned and
     complicated mind is the source of calamity.
He who leads others with simplicity is the source of blessing.

To know these two principles is to possess
     a rule and measure, the symbol of the ancient wise one.
To keep the rule and measure constantly in your mind,
     is to spontaneously manifest integral virtue.
Deep and far-reaching is the subtle truth of integrity.
It leads all things to return from worldly divergence
     to one great and universal life.

SIXTY-SIX

How does the sea
become the queen of all rivers and streams?
By lying lower than they do!
Hence, it is the queen of all rivers and streams.

One who humbles himself, therefore,
can serve all people.
By putting himself last, he comes to be their leader.
Thus, when one of subtle virtue is set above people,
they do not feel that he is their burden.
And, when he stands in front of people,
they do not feel that he is an obstruction to them.
Therefore, the world follows one of subtle virtue joyfully,
and never tires of doing so.
He does not compete with anyone,
thus he is above all competition.

SIXTY-SEVEN

*The world may say that the subtle Way of the universe
    which I describe is great,
  but that it has little bearing on worldly life.
Truly, it is just that it is not definable,
  like the small ways of the world,
  thus it is indeed great.*

*There are three treasures
  which I embrace and follow closely:
  the first is to be kind;
  the second is to be simple;
  the third is to not put one's own importance
  first in the world.*

*Because kindness and compassion
  can produce courage,
  simplicity can thus be broadened
  to contain the world.
By not putting your own importance first in worldly affairs,
  you will not impede the natural growth of all things.*

If a person endeavors to be brave without first being kind,
great purposed, without first simplifying his life,
an authority, without first denying himself,
he cannot evolve freely from strife,
and is only courting destruction.

Kindness can help to win a war.
Kindness can help to defend a fortification.
Kindness will invite the corresponding energy of
kindness from Heaven through all the divine beings
who support and protect.

SIXTY-EIGHT

A *good warrior is never violent.*
   A good fighter is never offensive.
A great victor defeats his opponent,
   but not by challenging him.
A great commander is humble.
This is called the power of non-contention.
This is also called making use of the effort of others.
To follow this is to follow the pattern
   of the subtle law of the universe.

SIXTY-NINE

The strategist who has achieved excellence says:
    dare not to be the host,
  but rather be the guest.
Dare not to be the restless aggressor,
    but rather be the calm defender.
Dare not advance an inch, but rather retreat a foot.

March forward where there is no obstacle.
Stretch out your arm
    only where there is no confrontation.
Charge an opponent where there is no resistance.
Hold a weapon that is invisible.

There is no greater mistake
    than to underestimate the power of an opponent.
To underestimate the power of an opponent
    may cost a man his life.
Therefore, when opposing troops meet in battle,
    it is the side with the greatest caution that wins.

SEVENTY

My words are very easy to understand
and easy to practice,
yet the world can neither understand
nor practice them.
My words have only one source:
the subtle truth of the universe.
My deeds have only one master:
the natural virtue of the universe.
The people of the world have no knowledge of this.
Thus, they have no knowledge of me.
The fewer the persons that know me,
the nobler are they that follow me.
Therefore, the one of whole virtue
wears coarse clothes superficially,
but holds a precious treasure within.

SEVENTY-ONE

*H*e *who regards his intellectual knowledge*
*   as ignorance has deep insight.*
He who overrates his intellectual achievement
*   as definite truth is deeply sick.*
Only when one is sick of this sickness
*   can one cease to be sick.*
One who returns his mind to the simplicity
*   of the subtle truth*
*   is not sick.*
He knows to break through conceptual knowledge
*   in order to directly reach*
*   the subtle truth of the universe.*
This is the foundation of his health!

SEVENTY-TWO

*When people lack a sense of pure spiritual piety
     toward natural life,
then awful things happen in their life.
Therefore, respect where you dwell.
Love your life and livelihood.
Because you do not disparage
     your life and livelihood,
     you will never become tired of life.*

*Thus, one of natural whole virtue respects his own life,
     but is not egotistical.
He loves his life, but does not exalt himself.
He holds a sense of spiritual serenity for all things,
     and disparages nothing.
Hence, he does what is right
     and gives up what is not right.*

SEVENTY-THREE

*H*e who is brave in daring
      will meet an unnatural death.
He who is brave in gentleness will be preserved.
Of these two kinds of bravery, one is beneficial,
      while the other proves harmful.
The subtle truth of the universe does not support
      those who are brave in daring,
      yet there are still many people
      who do not understand such apparent truth.
So, even the one who integrates his being
      with the subtle essence of the universe,
      dares not make light of the subtle law of life.

The subtle Way of the universe
      gave birth to a world of peace and order.
It responds to the order and harmony
      of all beings and things
      without needing to talk to them.
Without your summoning it, it comes to you.
Without scheming, its plan is perfect.
Vast is the subtle energy network of the universe.
Sparsely meshed it is, yet nothing can slip through it!

SEVENTY-FOUR

*If people are not afraid to die,
    what is the use of threatening them
    with the punishment of death?
On the other hand, if people value their lives,
    and if outlaws are seized and killed
    or are killed by what they are doing,
    who would dare risk a life of peace
    for the sake of an insecure future?*

*Yet it is always true
    that one who takes charge of killing is killed in turn.
To become the executioner of artificial righteousness
    is like the inexperienced lad
    who would brandish a sharp axe
    of a master carpenter.
He can seldom escape cutting himself.*

SEVENTY-FIVE

*W*hy are people starving and leading a difficult life?
    Is it not because their rulers
consume too much tax grain?
Is that why they are starving and leading a difficult life?

Why are people hard to manage?
Is it not because those above them
    create distress with their oppressive interference?
Is that why they are hard to manage?
Why do people make light of death?
Is it not because those above them
    demand too much for themselves
    and value only their own personal power and glory?
Is that why they take death so lightly?

One who is a guardian of people
    and does nothing for his own life
    knows how to value all lives well.

SEVENTY-SIX

*W*hen a person is alive, he is soft and supple.
When a person dies, he becomes hard and rigid.
When a plant is alive, it is pliant and tender.
When a plant is dead, it becomes dry and brittle.
Hence, the hard and rigid are companions of the dead.
The soft and supple are companions of the living.

Therefore, a mighty army is ready to be vanquished.
A tree that is dry is ready for the ax.
The mighty and the great will be laid low.
The soft and the gentle will outlive them all!

SEVENTY-SEVEN

*T*he subtle Way of the universe:
    is it not expressed in the stretching of a bow?
The high it presses down.
The low it lifts up.
The excessive it takes from.
The deficient it gives to.
It is the nature of this subtle truth to take
    from what is excessive and give to what is deficient.

The way of man, however, is otherwise.
It takes from those in need
    to give to those who already have more than enough.
Only one of whole virtue
    always has something to give to others.

Therefore, one of whole virtue does things,
    but does not keep them for himself;
    accomplishes his tasks, but does not cling to them.
He has no desire to trade his virtue for people's worship.

SEVENTY-EIGHT

*Nothing in the world is softer or more yielding
    than water.
But, for wearing down the hard and strong,
    there is nothing like it.
That yielding overcomes the strong
    and softness overcomes the hard
    is something that is known by all,
    but is practiced by few.*

*An ancient developed one said:
    "He who can take the troubles
    of the people of the world
    is qualified to rule the world.
    He who can tend to calamities for the sake of all beings
    is the right person to be the sovereign of the world."
Indeed, truth seems paradoxical!*

SEVENTY-NINE

*Even after settling a great dispute,
    some resentment is likely to remain.
Can this be considered a true settlement?*

*Only by cultivating the virtue of wholeness
    and by returning injury with kindness
    can there be true harmony.
Therefore, one of deep virtue always gives
    without expecting gratitude.*

*One whose virtue is deep treats the world
    as if he were the debtor,
    holding the left side of the tally.
He willingly repays the world
    through serving his fellow man.
One who is partially virtuous treats the world as if he
    were the creditor, holding the right side of the tally.
He thinks the world owes him something
    and should repay him.
Although the subtle Way of the universe
    holds no favoritism or partiality,
    it always supports those who are naturally virtuous.*

EIGHTY

*L*et *there be small communities with few inhabitants.*
   The supply of vessels may be more than enough,
   yet no one would use them.
The inhabitants would love living there so dearly
   that they would never wish to move to another place.
They may have every kind of vehicle,
   but they would not bother to ride them.
They may have powerful weapons,
   but they would not resort to using them.
They would return to a simple system of cords and knots
   to record their simple events,
   as was done in ancient times.
They would be content with plain food, pleased with
   simple clothing, satisfied with rustic but cozy homes,
   and would cling to their natural way of life.
The neighboring country would be so close at hand
   that one could hear its roosters crowing
   and its dogs barking along the boundaries.
But, to the end of their days, people would rarely
   trespass the territory of another's life.

EIGHTY-ONE

True words are not necessarily beautiful.
Beautiful words are not necessarily truthful.
One who is achieved does not argue,
and one who argues is not achieved.
One who knows the deepest truth
does not need segmented information.
One who knows vast amounts of information
may not know the truth.

One of deep virtue
is not occupied with amassing material goods,
yet the more he lives for others,
the richer his life becomes.
The more he gives, the more his life abounds.
The subtle Way of the universe is beneficial, not harmful.
The integral nature of a person
is to extend one's virtue unconditionally
and to contend with no one.

化胡經

Hua Hu Ching

INTRODUCTION TO
HUA HU CHING

F ew people are aware that after having imparted the
teachings of the *Tao Teh Ching*, as he traveled Lao Tzu
continued to share his teachings with those who sincerely
sought the high guidance of life from him. His essential
instruction was to live according to the Universal Integral
Way of balance and harmony. Only one known compila-
tion of those later teachings survived, and even it was
destroyed. It has come to be known as the *Hua Hu Ching*.

When Manichaeism, the religion created by the Syrian
religious leader Mani (215-274 C.E.), knocked on the door
of China, its source was identified as Lao Tzu's *Hua Hu
Ching*. Several versions of *Hua Hu Ching* may have
appeared. This one is my own education from my parents.
The writing is my personal attainment.

After the Mongolian invasion, the Yuan Dynasty was
established. The refined culture of the inland was devastat-
ed by the horse people. Emperor Shuen Ti (1333 C.E.-1367
C.E.) was persuaded by jealous and prejudiced religious
leaders of his own tribe of the border to ban the *Hua Hu
Ching* and order all copies of it to be burned. Certain
Buddhists in China felt that their spiritual leader Sakyamuni
was degraded by the *Hua Hu Ching*, because people often
associated him with the prince who is Lao Tzu's student in
the book. This association was doubtlessly inaccurate,
since in ancient times there were so many kingdoms that
kings and queens, princes and princesses were as numerous as grains of sand on a beach. The Prince could
therefore have been any learned noble.

The influence of the *Hua Hu Ching* can certainly be
seen in the teachings of Mahayana Buddhism, although it
is inaccurately interpreted as *prajna* (wisdom, which is the

doctrine of emptiness). The influence of the *Hua Hu Ching*
is also seen in the teachings of Sufism. However, the
teachings of Lao Tzu and the principles of the *I Ching*
elevated the new teaching of Buddhism as Mahayana
when more translations of these works from the influence
of northern culture moved west and south. After being
reedited, it went back to China. In the same period, Ch'an
(Zen) Buddhism in China produced several important
Buddhist books said to be Sakyamuni's teaching such as
the Lani Sutra (楞嚴經), the Sutra of Full Awakening
(.圓覺經) and a particular philosophical discussion
called the Introduction to Mahayana (大乘起信論),
etc. These three were the most influential in making
Buddhism part of Chinese culture. Thus Ch'an Buddhism is
actually an ancient Taoist teaching cloaked in Buddhist
garments which afterwards spread to Japan and Korea.

Manichaeism was absorbed by Tibetan Buddhism and
folk Taoism. Some teachings of Zoroaster and Mani can be
found in a reedited form as the Pure Land School of
Mahayana Buddhism which was widely practiced in China.
You can find influences of Lao Tzu and the *Book of
Changes* in many of these teachings.

Cultural integration and the replacement of old religions by new ones is unavoidable as societies form and
reform. New teachers always tailor their teachings for a
new generation of people. Christianity is one such reediting of Greek philosophy and the virtuous conviction of
Socrates with Jesus as the projection of such a combination.

All culture is based on the past. For example, Judaism
is the reediting of Egyptian and Babylonian culture, and
Islam is the reediting of Judaism and Christianity. Chinese
culture draws upon the *I Ching*, which is derived from the
simple inspiration of nature. To see the simple symbols *Hu
Tu* and *Lu Su* please refer to my work *The Natural
Paradigm of the Universe*.

According to scholars, there were several versions of
the *Hua Hu Ching*. The collection of Dunhuang Caves in
Gansu province dating from 366 C.E. contains Buddhist

statues, frescoes and valuable manuscripts, including the name *Hua Hu Ching*. The preface of the *Hua Hu Ching* and a few scattered chapters were also kept in the *Taoist Canon,* which was compiled during the Ming Dynasty (1368-1643 C.E.). However, the *Hua Hu Ching* may no longer exist in China. Few, if any, complete and accurate copies of it exist today. It is only through the oral transmission of its teachings, generation after generation, by highly developed individuals that Lao Tzu's teachings have been preserved. Until now, the *Tao Teh Ching* has been the only work by Lao Tzu available to the public.

Truth itself is power. By using and persistently studying this book, many kinds of help can be obtained. The teachings of Lao Tzu point to and reveal the highest dimension of life that is the original focus and inspiration for all religions. Its highest value, however, is the guidance to abide by the natural subtle law of the universe that I have expounded in *Tao, the Subtle Universal Law.*

The shell of a book can be burned by those who have not attained any spiritual development, but no one can damage the subtle truth that is beyond any form. For this reason, this precious teaching has now reached you.

This book represents my education as a youth. I was the *hu* or individual who needed to be civilized spiritually through a broad spiritual education. The contents of this version present the integral truth that is indivisible. No single religion is enough to carry the whole truth of universal spiritual reality, which must be whole or nothing. Every human creation has made a contribution to the unfolding truth of wholeness. Thus what I have presented here is not a segmented religious teaching, but the ageless universal inspiration for all people.

The material in this book is more than a translation, it is an elucidation drawing upon my decades of spiritual cultivation and training in this tradition. Anyone who wishes to produce their own version of this material should work directly from an original text rather than copying from my work.

老君曰：大道無形，常居杳冥，隨機化物，以應精誠，子能寂念，受吾真經，能持受者，口淨神清，然後誦之，萬惡不生，可以治病，可以度厄，百邪不干，群妖束形，所以然者，一切含靈，皆具本真，一經受化，達本逍遙．明真出因，今於其中，化煉心身，掃蕩散亂，滌除雜染，三業常淨，六情了澄，五神守護，三一長存，朝夕兩時，依經返照，坐臥安穩，魂魄康寧，耳聰目明，身強體輕，唯精唯一，返樸還真，不入生死，永為仙真．

ONE

There once was a great white-bearded master who
appeared at the boundary of the Central Territory[1] on
his journey west. Followers came from everywhere to sit at
his feet, for he was a model of universal harmony. His
teaching was simple, yet profound. His instruction was
neither ordinary religion nor worldly wisdom, yet it revealed
the truth of every aspect of the universe. All of his friends and
followers lived virtuously and performed whatever work
came to them joyfully. They maintained a peaceful, righteous way of life and enjoyed the abundance of their being.
After their daily work was completed, they cleansed themselves carefully and fed themselves properly. Then they
went to the garden where the old master stayed and awaited
his precious instruction.

TWO

On the occasion of one such gathering, a wise disciple
who was the prince of the country rose among the
group and humbly saluted the master, saying, "Venerable
master of the world, one who is virtuous without discrimination takes care of those who practice virtue and selflessness.
One who is virtuous without discrimination also guides
those who do not practice virtue and selflessness. Please
instruct us. How should men and women who are motivated
to attain correct awareness of their true nature calm their
minds? What path should they follow in order to attune their
minds harmoniously to all aspects of life?"

[1] In ancient times, this term was used to refer to the country that is known
as China today. The actual event could have happened somewhere near Kashmir,
where there were many small tribes and kingdoms. The teaching of the Hua Hu
Ching may have inspired the development of some part of Mahayana Buddhism.

The old master said, "One of virtue and wholeness takes care of those who practice virtue and selflessness. One of virtue and wholeness also guides those who do not practice virtue and selflessness, as you said.

"Please listen well. Any good person who is motivated to attain awareness of the whole truth should follow the Universal Integral Way to calm his mind and harmonize it with all aspects of life."

The prince said gladly, "Most Venerable Master, we are ready to receive your precious guidance with great joy."

THREE

The master told the prince and all the followers, "All of my friends and disciples should attune their minds to all life and hold no antagonism toward any living thing whether it be born of womb, egg, moisture or any other kind of transformation; whether it can think or is unable to think; whether it has form or is formless. You should dissolve all discrimination of individuality and absorb all things into a harmonious oneness. All lives are one life that can be called the One Great Universal Life.

"Virtue is developed by highly evolved people who embrace all people and things and dispel the darkness which isolates them. Although innumerable lives are illuminated, highly evolved people do not think they have helped anyone, because to them the world is synonymous with oneself and one's self is the world. One who is aware of the whole really helps others. Why is this so? Kind prince, if one still holds the divisive mental concepts of self and others, male and female, longevity and brevity, life and death, and so on without end, then one does not have an all-embracing awareness of the Universal Life."

FOUR

The master continued, "One who practices virtue and selflessness should not hold any particular idea in his mind about how to fulfill his virtue, for virtue is the very nature of one's being. One should always be willing to assist others selflessly and unconditionally by offering one's skills and achievements to serve them. One should be willing to give away the things one cherishes most and even offer one's life to assist others.

"One should not restrict one's service by making distinctions based on color, nationality, family or social relationships, sensory perceptions or any other relative conditions. To restrict the ways in which one would render service to others in order to suit one's personal preference is potentially harmful.

"Kind prince, if one relates to others and serves them only according to his own design, it is as if he had entered darkness and was blind. He might help some people by chance and he might also injure some, but if one does not limit oneself by imposing special terms on his service, then he is like a person with good vision who sees clearly and whose influence is purely positive.

"Following the Universal Way of life means practicing selflessness and extending virtue to the world unconditionally. In this way one not only eliminates the heavy contamination accumulated throughout many lifetimes, but may also bring about the possibility of restoring one's original divine nature and becoming an integral being of the multi-universe. This is the only way to dissolve the self-created agony, misery and tragedy that are experienced in one's life.

"Every expression of life is the reality of life. One's every movement and activity evoke a response from the subtle energy of the universe. When one does not limit himself by imposing conditions on rendering service to others, the blessings evoked will also be limitless."

FIVE

The old master said, "Kind prince, what do you think? Can the great space of the East be measured by the mind?"
The prince replied, "No, Venerable Teacher."

"Kind prince, what do you think? Can the space of the four directions, as well as above and below, which constitute the profound vastness of the universe, be measured by the mind?"

"No, Venerable Teacher."

"Kind prince, the mind can be just as immeasurable as the universe itself. An integral being settles his mind just as the vast universe settles itself. He unites his mind with the unnameable Subtle Origin and its expression as the multi-universe in which there is no past, present or future. This is how an integral being deals with his mind."

SIX

"Kind prince," asked the old master, "what do you think? Can the subtle cosmic body of the Universal One be seen in any beautiful form?"

"No, Venerable Teacher," replied the prince, "the subtle cosmic body of the Universal One cannot be seen in any beautiful form, because to the Universal One there is nothing which can be considered as form."

"Kind prince, as soon as the Universal One is mentioned people immediately formulate images in their imaginations. Then they try to make reality conform to their imaginary concepts. The Universal One is truly imageless, yet in the attempt to make it conform to an image, people distort its reality and separate themselves from it."

SEVEN

The prince inquired of the master, "Venerable Teacher, will there be people in the future who will have the opportunity to learn and follow the Universal Integral Way of Life by studying these bamboo scrolls on which your great teachings are recorded?"

The master told him, "Kind prince, please do not wonder about this. After I depart, even many, many generations later, if there are still people who seek the Integral Way, they will receive this precious guidance.

"Those who seek and attain the Way must have planted their roots and virtue in one or two or even five lifetimes. Actually, they have already evolved to a very high level. Thus, when they learn the truth contained in these teachings, their hearts may immediately reconnect with the integral nature of the multi-universe. Then the omniscient, omnipresent Integral One, which is the Treasure of Divine Power of the multi-universe, will shine upon them and absorb them into its radiance. They will become submerged in the boundless ocean of blessings and impersonal love of the Universal One.

"Why is this so? Those people will have dissolved their rigid concepts of self and others, male and female, longevity and brevity, life and death. Also, they will not have any mental obstructions formed by different cultural backgrounds, customs or religious beliefs which would prevent the perception of the subtle truth of universal integration. To hold the mind within any rigid framework is to immediately become trapped in the bondage of duality. If one does not discriminate between what is labeled as sacred and profane, one is liberated from the bondage of all concepts. Thus one should not embrace any religious concept or mental structure that is formed while living in the physical world. All mental structures must finally be relinquished if one is to reach the ultimate and subtle truth of oneness."

EIGHT

The master said, "Kind prince, what do you think? Has the Universal One invented something to teach us?"

"No, Venerable Teacher," replied the prince, "the Universal One has invented nothing to teach."

"Kind prince, what do you think? Have I attained an awareness which is beyond the integral truth? Have I established a personal teaching which is separate from the Universal Way?"

"Venerable Teacher, according to my understanding, there is nothing definite or set which can lead one to reach the integral truth. Nor is unconditioned awareness a set or rigid way of perceiving things. All true guidance is intangible because the Universal Integral Way is beyond the limits of the mind. The Universal Way is neither religious nor worldly. All of the far-reaching, unfaded teachings of the ancient sages come from the same source: the subtle truth of great oneness. Different expressions are merely the result of different times and places."

NINE

"What do you think, kind prince?" asked the master. "Suppose a person amasses a worldly treasure and then gives it all away to those in need. According to the universal law of energy response, will he derive blessings in proportion to the treasure he gives away?"

"Yes, Venerable Teacher, there will be abundant blessings derived from this."

"Kind prince, if someone cherishes the guidance of these teachings, uses it to instruct others and serve them selflessly, the blessings of this person will be far greater than those of the former. Why is this?"

"Venerable Teacher, if one amasses wealth and gives it

away in the hope of receiving blessings, he earns his blessings by striving and therefore struggles with the duality of the mental realm. The one who practices the Universal Way and then guides others gives spontaneously whatever he has, simply because it is his nature to do so; thus he derives his blessings through non-action and never deviates from the Universal Way."

"Kind prince, true blessings and impersonal love are beyond the concept of measurement. When we start to be concerned about blessings, they cease to be blessings."

TEN

"Kind prince," said the master, "suppose a person cuts himself loose from being fooled by the senses. Can he then become attached to the fruit of his enlightenment?"

"No, Venerable Teacher. The one who has succeeded in cutting himself loose from attachment to the senses cannot then fasten himself to what he has attained. To do so would be to return to the enslavement of the senses, and the reign of the ego would ruin what he had attained. Therefore, one cannot hold any idea in the mind about what one has attained."

"What do you think, kind prince? Suppose a person discovers that his life has been a ceaseless pattern of coming and going. Suppose further that he decides to make this journey his last and sets out to accomplish the final purification in order to live forever in the Realm of Universal Life. Can he become attached to the idea of the culmination of his final journey?"

"No, he cannot, Venerable Teacher. The one who discovers that life is a phenomenon of coming and going also discovers that there is no such thing as coming and going at the root of integral life. How, then, could he become attached to what is called the last journey of life?"

"Then, kind prince, what do you think? Can one who

has achieved the state of desireless happiness presume to
have finally reached the state of desirelessness? Or can one
who has transcended life and death to enjoy the Universal
Way be happy about his attainment?"

"No, Venerable Teacher. One who has already attained
final transcendence would not think of having transcended
life and death. The concepts of life and death would only
trap him again in the bondage of duality with its mental
framework of self and others, longevity and brevity, life and
death.

"Venerable Teacher, you have attested that I have
purified myself so thoroughly that no desire or conflict
remain and that I have attained the highest possible level of
virtue. Yet I never think about having no desires. Because I
do not hold anything particular in my mind, I am on the
Universal Integral Way. To be completely desireless is to
achieve the true happiness of agelessness; it is the way of
transcendental bliss."

ELEVEN

The master said, "Kind prince, what do you think? When
I was a pupil at my master's side, did I learn anything
from my master that would make me feel sanctimonious?"

"No, Venerable Teacher, you learned nothing that
would make you feel sanctimonious."

"Well then, kind prince, what do you think? Is the
residence of the Universal One very sublime?"

"No, Venerable Teacher, where the Universal One
resides cannot be defined in that manner. If it could be
defined in that manner, it would not be the achievement of
total integration which cannot be touched by a fragmented
mind. Yet it may be called the Life of the Most Sublime.
Therefore, one should keep one's mind pure, simple, plain
and untouched. One should not disintegrate one's mind by
creating dualistic concepts of different forms, sounds, smells,

flavors, feelings, or anything else that fosters the illusion of separation. In order to reach complete integration, one must dedicate one's being wholly to the integral truth."

"Tell me, kind prince," said the master, "if someone's body were as big as the Mountain of Enormity, do you think his body would be very large?"

"It would be huge, Venerable Teacher. But why do you ask such a question?"

"Kind prince, the formless body of integral truth is immeasurably vast, and yet is also immeasurably small! Small and large are both conceivable, but can you cease thinking? The simple, natural reality is the same whether you think of it as large or as small."

TWELVE

The master continued his instruction. "Kind prince, if there were as many rivers in the world as there are grains of sand in the River of Timelessness, and if each river contained as much sand as the River of Timelessness, do you think that would be a vast amount of sand?"

"Yes, indeed, Venerable Teacher; it would be very vast."

"Kind prince, if a person amassed a huge fortune and gave it all away to help as many people as there are grains of sand in the River of Timelessness, would the blessing that he gained be as great as what he gave?"

"It would be very great indeed, Venerable Teacher, because returning an equivalent response is the nature of the subtle law of the universe."

"That is true, kind prince, but if one practiced the truth contained in these teachings and expounded it to others, the benevolent grace and blessings he would evoke from the universe would be even greater. When someone elucidates this sacred scripture to others, the place in which he does so becomes sacred and is respected by all spiritual beings, those with form as well as those without. Wherever these teachings are, the Sacred Altar is. All the virtuous beings of the universe pay homage to it, and the divine guardians of the eight powerful energy rays protect it. All people should reverently offer salutations and incense to it and surround it with fragrant flowers.

"Furthermore, if someone embraces the integral truth contained in this scripture, and studies and practices it, then he must attain the highest blessing of all beings. All of the great masters of the Universal Way respond to those who cherish it. Is this thinkable? Why should people live within the smallness of the mind?"

THIRTEEN

"Kind prince," asked the master, "what do you think? Are all the small particles that make up the universe numerous?"

"Yes, very numerous, Venerable Teacher."

"And, kind prince, do you think the universe is very vast?"

"It is vast indeed, Venerable Teacher."

"But, kind prince, the Universal Truth is that the particles are not small, nor is the universe vast. It is merely the relative mind that labels them so.

"Kind prince, what do you think? Can one imagine the Universal One as having any kind of wonderful form?"

"No, Venerable Teacher, one cannot imagine the Universal One as having any kind of wonderful form, because to the Universal One form is not real; it is merely labeled as such."

"Now, kind prince, if there are good men and women who offer their lives in service to others, their blessings will certainly be bountiful. But if someone practices the truth contained in the lines and chapters of this scripture, and expounds it to others, his blessings will be immeasurably and inconceivably abundant."

FOURTEEN

At that time the prince wholly understood the wonderful teaching that the master had given him. He could not help bursting into tears with deep sadness for his past ignorance, and he said, "Venerable Teacher, this is the most profound instruction I have heard since I first began developing my own insight. It is truly the highest teaching. I am deeply grateful to you for your instruction and I vow to practice this truth joyfully as the sacred fulfillment of my life.

"I wonder, though, if many generations from now, there will be people who will discover this instruction and be able to practice it joyfully in their daily lives. If so, these individuals would be most unusual, for they would have dissolved all mental concepts of ego, self and others, male and female, longevity and brevity, and life and death. Those who dissolve all concepts of individuality are beings of absolute awareness. By regaining Oneness with the clarity of their minds, they would fulfill the most virtuous merit and attain the highest blessing."

"Very true, kind prince. If someone in the future embraces this revelation of the integral life without skepticism, conflict or panic, then this person would be very, very unusual.

"Kind prince, if we label the Universal Truth as subtle and transcendental, then it ceases to be true integral Oneness. By doing this, we reduce it to the mental sphere of dichotomy where it is no longer the essential, direct and undistorted reflection of the universal truth of one life."

FIFTEEN

The master continued, "Kind prince, tolerance is a necessary virtue in everyone's daily life, but for a universal integral being there is nothing that needs to be tolerated or labeled as tolerance. Tolerance exists only in the relative sphere.

"Why is this? If someone does something unpleasant to us, we need to gather our strength to bear it; it is a difficult and disagreeable situation. However, if you have risen above the relative concepts of the mind, there is no self and others, no longevity or brevity, no life or death in your mind, so there is no hatred or resentment. What, then, is the necessity for tolerance?

"Kind prince, a person who is highly evolved leaves behind all concepts of individuality and extends impersonal love to include all existence. Dissolving individuality enables one to free oneself from the entangling discriminations of form, language, sense perception, feeling and all other relative conditions. It allows one's true being to grow freely without the hindrance of attachment. When the mind is attached to something, it can hold little more than self-created pain. One who is highly evolved, therefore, is attached to nothing and does not depend on any particular mental concept or form in his relations with people or in serving them. His very being benefits all life.

"To a universal being all form is equal to that which is formless. All life is equal to all non-life. Kind prince, this is the reality of the universe; it is the subtle integral truth and not a religious invention. There is no need for further commentary, for the instruction of transcendental, central reality is beyond the realm of truism and falseness in ordinary logic. Only the individual who has already evolved to a high level may receive this precious instruction."

SIXTEEN

"Kind prince, suppose there are good men and women who offer as much of themselves as there is sand in the River of Timelessness to help people in the morning, and as much of themselves as there is sand in the River of

Timelessness to help people in the afternoon, and then as much of themselves as there is sand in the River of Timelessness to help people in the evening. Suppose, too, that they continue to do this for eon after eon for the purpose of receiving virtuous blessings.

"Now suppose there are people who hear this sacred scripture and joyfully break through all obstacles in order to follow it. The blessings of these people will be even greater yet, for this scripture has boundless power.

"The Universal One reveals the truth contained in this scripture to those who cultivate themselves not for their own sake, nor only half for their sake and half for others. The Universal One reveals this profundity to those who cultivate themselves for the sake of all, for this is the highest level of virtue. If there is someone who accepts this truth and who studies, practices and teaches it widely, then this person will certainly be acknowledged by the universal beings of the divine realm. This person will truly accomplish the great merit of shouldering the responsibility of transmitting the divine revelation.

"Kind prince, many people are pleased and satisfied with the various limited religious doctrines existing in the world today. They all hope to live in the kingdom of Heaven someday and sit sublimely at the side of their personal deity, but by entertaining such hopes and beliefs they only foster concepts of self and others, longevity and brevity, life and death, and so on without end. With such conceptual entanglements they cannot even listen to the truth, much less study, practice and embrace it or explain it to others. In this case, how can they ever uplift themselves to the subtle, central realm to be with the Universal One of One Universal Life?"

SEVENTEEN

The master continued, "Kind prince, if good men and women study and embrace this scripture, yet are scorned by others, this is the result of the ignorant actions of their past lives that are bearing bad fruit in this life. Through continuing to study and practice the truth contained in this scripture, however, their energy will be cleansed and they will attain the crystal clear awareness of a universal being.

"Kind prince, after I received my birth from the Subtle Origin, I dedicated myself through many lifetimes to innumerable religions and their deities, believing that they would act as intermediaries between me and the subtle, integral reality of the universe. I did not neglect or overlook a single one of them. Yet, if someone in the distant future, in the Age of Confusion for instance, were to directly embrace the integral truth contained in this scripture, the virtue he would embody and the merit he would attain would be much, much greater than what I attained through my long religious dedication. This is because he would be aware of his own divine nature through direct contact with it, not through the indirect process of worshiping others who have achieved the integral truth.

"Those who turn to deities as intermediaries between themselves and the subtle truth are like beggars who look outside themselves for the very treasure contained within their own nature. It is only after one discovers one's own divine nature that prayer or any form of worshiping the one universal life can be a true and effective spiritual cultivation of the wholeness of eternal life.

"Kind prince, as I just mentioned, if there are good people in the future who can embrace the truth contained in this scripture and who can study and practice it with great sincerity, the merit and virtue they will attain shall be immeasurable. You see, kind prince, this scripture is the subtle truth of one integral universal life, and the responsive power of the Universal Integral Way neglects no one and can be denied by no one!"

EIGHTEEN

At that time the prince asked the master again, "Venerable Teacher, if good men and women are motivated to attain correct awareness in order to restore their integral nature, how can they maintain this awareness and subdue the delusive activity of the mind?"

The master replied, "Kind prince, good people who are motivated to attain the correct awareness of a universal being should dissolve all conceptions of duality. With integral awareness of their moral responsibility, they will be able to help all people to eliminate the darkness of the dichotomous mind and the delusions stemming from concepts of existence and non-existence so that they can finally attain the essence of integral subtle transcendence. When this has been achieved, the one who renders service to others discovers that, in truth, there is no one being served; he no longer perceives other lives as external to himself, nor does he perceive his own existence as separate and individual. If universal beings still held any concepts of self and others, longevity and brevity, life and death, then they would not be beings of true universal awareness.

"Kind prince, what do you think? Did I attain awareness of the integral nature of the universe through the use of any special esoteric method?"

"No, Venerable Teacher," replied the prince, "As I understand, what you teach us is not something that can be obtained through the practice of any esoteric method, for there is no specific device that can uplift one to the higher realms. Once something is labeled as the ultimate method or device, it has already become a hindrance to one's attainment of integral awareness. Therefore, to an integral or universal being, any external established means is not the Universal Way."

"You are right, kind prince. There truly is no way for a Universal One to separate his being from the nature of the universe. If I had used any particular way to attain awareness of the integral nature of the universe, then the masters who live in the deep central realm of one great life would not have recognized me as a universal being. They refer to me, however, as a cosmic person who lives in all times and places, and this is what a universal being should be.

"If there is someone who states that a Universal One has attained the correct awareness of the integral nature of the universe by means of any specific way, then he is simply mistaken. There is no relative, specific way in which one can achieve awareness of the integral truth. The integral truth of the universe cannot be distinguished through a dualistic mode of perception. Therefore, a Universal One teaches only the integral way of life. What are labeled as methods of achieving enlightenment and uplifting one to the higher realms, wise prince, do not exist in the integral realm.

"Kind prince, one of integral virtue is selfless and impartial. When my fellow students and I studied with our teacher, no one received special attention or instruction for his own particular benefit. The teacher gave the same instruction to all of us and it was up to each student to absorb, digest and develop the teaching within himself. A student should not attempt to provoke special attention or instruction from his teacher, nor should he attempt to sway the teacher to show a personal preference for him. Some people try very hard to impress a deity in whom they believe in order to invoke special favors or blessings, but this is only a fantasy that demonstrates the person's lack of true spiritual development. Unconditional sincerity is what evokes a response from the subtle realm of universal divine power.

"For a teacher to impart his wisdom to others is purely a realization of his virtue. A student should not try to disturb his teacher with emotional or material entanglements of any kind, because the gross energy of mental, physical or emotional entanglement severs the subtle spiritual connection with the divine energy. If a disciple is excessively emotional or if his mind is very rigid, good teachings will be distorted and the teacher's wisdom will not be assimilated. If the teacher must continually work on the student's mental problems, he is prevented from sharing his spiritual treasure with the student. The student should not insist that the teacher solve his problems or do the inner work that is an essential aspect of one's own cultivation. Instead, the student should eliminate all obstacles and make himself an empty vessel to receive the light of One Great Life from his teacher."

NINETEEN

"Kind prince," asked the master, "how do we recognize the size of the body which humankind possesses?"

The prince replied, "Venerable Teacher, according to the Universal Way, the big body possessed by humankind is not big but is merely called so. It is not bigger or smaller than any other kind of life."

"Kind prince, this understanding is the foundation of correct awareness. If a person says that he should help all people by sharing his correct awareness with them, he shows that he does not truly have correct awareness. Why is this? An integral universal being has no perception of self and others, life and death, longevity and brevity. If there is no self, there are no others to help through sharing one's awareness.

"Kind prince, if one of correct awareness states that the temple is holy and sublime, he does not truly have correct awareness because a universal being labels nothing. People may label a temple as holy and sublime by creating the dualistic concept of places which are holy and sublime in contrast to places which are not. Only when one has dissolved all discrimination, however, can he be recognized as having attained correct awareness of integralness. Kind prince, ignore all appearances of duality and embrace only the integral, one universal life."

TWENTY

"Kind prince, what do you think?" asked the master. "Does the Universal One have physical eyes?"

"Yes, Venerable Teacher, the Universal One has physical eyes."

"What do you think, kind prince? Does the Universal One have spiritual eyes?"

"Indeed, Venerable Teacher, the Universal One has spiritual eyes which can see through all things."

"Kind prince, what do you think? Has the Universal One special eyes of wisdom?"

"Yes, Venerable Teacher, the Universal One has eyes of wisdom."

"Kind prince, what do you think? Does the Universal One have unusual eyes which discern all kinds of spiritual paths?"

"Yes, Venerable Teacher, the Universal One has outstanding eyes which can perceive all things and all spiritual paths."

"Kind prince, does the Universal One have integral eyes?"

"Yes, Venerable Teacher, the Universal One has integral eyes that are incomparable to all other eyes."

"Kind prince, people with clairvoyance may see things that are not within sight, but they cannot see the formless. People with clairaudience may hear special sounds, but they cannot hear the soundless. People with telepathy may communicate directly with another being's mind, but they cannot communicate with people who have achieved no-mind. People with telekinetic ability may move things without physically touching them, but they cannot move the intangible.

"Kind prince, all of these abilities exist only in the realm of duality. They lose their meaning before the Universal One, for to the Universal One there is nothing which can be called clairvoyance, clairaudience, telepathy or telekinesis. These are things that are merely labeled so."

TWENTY-ONE

"Kind prince, what do you think? Does the Universal One refer to the sand in the River of Timelessness as sand?"

"Yes, Venerable Teacher, the Universal One refers to the sand in the River of Timelessness as sand."

"Kind prince, what do you think? If there were as many rivers as there are grains of sand in the River of Timelessness, and if there were as many worlds as there are grains of sand in all the rivers, would that be very many?"

"Very many, indeed, Venerable Teacher."

"Kind prince, the sand is truly no different from the world, and the world is no different from the sand. People form their minds in countless ways and the Universal One knows all of them. How? To the Universal One the mind is not real. The mind of the past cannot be kept, the mind of the present cannot be held, and the mind of the future cannot be caught. Yet people are attached to such delusions and label them as mind.

"Kind prince, it is not the mind which varies constantly, but events which are ever changing. The events of the past cannot be kept, the events of the present cannot be held, and the events of the future cannot be caught. But the mind is too easily possessed by such images. If events themselves do not seize the mind and totally absorb one's consciousness, then the preconceptions and preoccupations of the mind prevent one from true awareness of the event. When these deviations occur trouble is sure to follow. An enjoyable past event cannot be held, and the bright future is delayed by one's anxiety. Beautiful present circumstances cannot be preserved. All good things seem fragile and fleeting. Dissolve attachment to these things and embrace only the Universal Truth. Universal awareness is not distant; clarity is close at hand."

TWENTY-TWO

The master said, "Kind prince, what do you think? Can the Universal One be seen as having a beautiful physical appearance?"

"No, Venerable Teacher, the Universal One cannot be seen as having a beautiful physical appearance because to the Universal One the possession of a beautiful form is equal to the possession of no form. It is only relatively named so."

"What do you think, then, kind prince? Does the Universal One present all kinds of wonders and preform miracles in order to show off his divine majesty or inspire faith and obedience in others?"

"No, Venerable Teacher, the Universal One does not present itself in that way, because to present wonders and perform miracles for such purposes is not its nature."

"Kind prince, the subtle body of the Universal One is omnipresent. It always exists, and it presents itself when all speech has been exhausted and the mind has been stripped away. When crystal clarity and unadulterated purity appear, the subtle body of the Universal One appears. When the highest sincerity is achieved, the subtle cosmic body of the Universal One responds. Then, wise prince, the Universal One can be seen even in what appears to be plain, simple and ordinary."

TWENTY-THREE

"Kind prince, please do not suppose that a universal being imposes any particular doctrine on people. If someone says that a universal being sets up a particular religious teaching to transmit the truth, he is ignorant of the Universal Way and does not truly understand what I have said. The most achieved of teachers actually has nothing to say. Although what he teaches may be called the highest truth, the reality can never be put into words."

At that time the prince asked the master, "Venerable Teacher, when people hear this truth in the future, will they be able to follow it?"

"Kind prince, do not worry about whether there will be people to follow it or not. An integral universal being knows that nothing which can be put into words is the integral truth. He does not ask people to follow, his only interest is to serve. He does not indulge in worry, but simply does his work. This is called 'doing that which is done by not-doing.'"

TWENTY-FOUR

The prince addressed the master once again. "Venerable Teacher, according to the Universal Way, when one attains subtle universal awareness he should not label it an achievement. Is that correct?"

The master kindly answered, "Yes, this is very true, dear prince. I have received nothing from the attainment of unconditional awareness. Awareness of the integral nature of the universe is indescribable; it cannot be contained by any word or name. If a person thinks in terms of attaining something, that means he believes there is something to obtain or achieve external to his own nature. It means that he fails to realize that his own true nature is the integral nature of the universe itself."

TWENTY-FIVE

The master continued, "Moreover, kind prince, the Universal One is revealed in the equality of the nature of all things. In reality, nothing is high or low. To be aware of this is to know the Universal Integral Way.

"When one has no awareness of self and others or of life and death and when one lives one's life with sincerity, then every moment and every activity are an expression of the bondage-free truth. It is no longer necessary to attain a transcendental awareness of the integral nature of the universe.

"Kind prince, all spiritual paths are not true paths that can lead one to the Universal Realm of universal oneness. People may call them spiritual, but in reality they are only mental constructs. Follow only the Universal Way that is above all words, embrace only the Oneness that is above all form, and ignore all divergence."

TWENTY-SIX

The prince was very much enlightened at this time and with great humility he said, "Venerable Teacher, your precious guidance has illuminated the two kinds of blessings: worldly blessings, which are planted by good deeds and alms giving and which are limited in time and space by the conditioned mind, and universal blessing, which is derived from the expression of universal or integral awareness in all aspects of life. This awareness frees one from the bondage of the conditioned body, mind and spirit. Once freed, one can emerge into the integral realm to live here and now. This blessing is boundless and unquestionable.

"Venerable Teacher, you have also illuminated the two kinds of wisdom. Worldly wisdom can help one understand worldly things, but it is only conceptual understanding and thus hinders the direct experience of the truth. Understanding always comes one moment after the experience itself and therefore cannot be direct enlightenment which dissolves both subject and object. While universal wisdom sometimes appears to be the opposite of worldly wisdom, it too can help connect one to worldly things, but in this case the connection of the mind with reality is not through any pattern of understanding but through direct participation in the experience of life. The observer and the object of observation are dissolved with no hindrance of preconception or delayed understanding. It is not necessary to accumulate mental attitudes after an experience has taken place, because to be is to know. This is the way of a universal being.

"Universal blessings and wisdom transcend all relative blessings and wisdom. If someone amasses a vast amount of wealth and gives it away to the needy, the blessing he can receive through this is tremendous, but such a blessing is only one zillionth of a zillionth the amount of blessing that is bestowed on one who practices and guides others to the Universal Way expounded in this scripture."

TWENTY-SEVEN

"Kind prince," said the master, "please do not think that a universal being holds the idea of conveying people to the integral realm. Why? Because there are no people to be conveyed to the integral realm.

"There is no 'self,' yet worldly people believe that a self exists. Wise prince, to a universal being so-called worldly people are not worldly, they are only titled so. Worldlings and immortals, the unaware and the enlightened, all originally have the same nature as the Subtle Path itself. There is not the slightest difference in their true nature."

TWENTY-EIGHT

"Kind prince," continued the master, "what do you think? Can one observe the appearance of the Universal One in all kinds of beautiful forms?"

"It could be so, Venerable Teacher. The appearance of the Universal One could be seen as the model of universal perfection."

"Kind prince, if one discerns the Universal One in all kinds of beautiful forms, then all the luminous heavenly bodies in the sky would be the subtle cosmic body of the

Universal One."

The prince then told the master, "Venerable Teacher, according to my present understanding of the Universal Integral Way, one should not mistake the subtle cosmic body of the Universal One as having form in the relative sense."

At that time, the master affirmed the prince's answer by saying: "If one sees the Universal One in a particular form; if one searches for the Universal One in a particular tone; such a person practices sorcery and can never see the subtle cosmic body of the Universal One."

TWENTY-NINE

"Kind prince," said the master, "if you think that an universal being attains total awareness without relying on relative practices and with no need of proper discipline or necessary rituals, then you have the wrong idea. My most important request is that you do not think that by giving up these postures, rituals, manners, disciplines and practices one can attain infinite awareness of the omnipresent truth. These things can help channel one's emotions as well as the total life energy itself. It can be an effective process of refinement for molding a beginner into the correct shape for life.

"Kind prince, do not misunderstand and think that one who has attained the highest, unconditional awareness should reject the natural, fundamental truth, common sense, definable practices, moral law, and virtuous conduct; this way of thinking will not lead to complete awareness but only to monomania or the worship of absolute authority. Being spiritual does not mean being disrespectful of the orderliness of society. Nor does it mean evading one's responsibilities or overlooking the basics of life, such as taking care of the young and the old and looking after one's marriage partner. One who is motivated to attain the highest universal awareness does not reject the practice of a simple, virtuous life, a healthy regimen and universal-mindedness. Without

good self-discipline, one falls apart again, loses the awareness he has attained and returns to the darkness he left
behind. Though the road to achievement is always open to
one who has been there, one cannot be sure of never falling
back again. There are many spiritual practitioners, therefore,
who are in a constant flux of up and down, never respecting
the consistency of good self-discipline.

"Wise prince, to practice all these essential disciplines is
to live the Universal Way of Life and the ultimate truth of
nature, beyond all relative principles and fragmentary ideas.
All the unnecessary beliefs and activities of worldly life
impair the well-being of an individual and spoil the peace
and harmony of human relations.

"Kind prince, one who follows the Universal Way helps
those who are spiritually undeveloped and who rely on
transitory, illusory images and methods before reaching the
ultimate truth. One who follows the Universal Integral Way
does not deny the importance of making the correct effort
to achieve a positive, plain, healthy and natural life. This is
because one who follows the Universal Integral Way does
not hold the erroneous view that life is merely an individual-
ized, physical phenomenon and that all consciousness
ceases at death.

"Wise prince, if one who practices virtue amasses
worldly treasures as numerous as the grains of sand in the
River of Timelessness and gives them as alms to the needy,
but another practices virtue in all aspects of life, selflessly
and with incomparable perseverance, the fulfillment of the
latter is so great it is unfathomable.

"Kind prince, virtuous beings never take advantage of
others, nor do they desire favor or reward for their virtuous
actions."

Then the prince asked the master, "Venerable Teacher,
why is it that those who are virtuous do not have the virtue
to accept blessings that are the result of their actions?"

"Kind prince, virtuous beings practice virtue without
any personal consideration. When I say that they do not
accept the rewards of their virtuous behavior, I mean that
they do nothing to spoil the unconditional quality of their

virtue. Thus, they are universal integral beings. In order to achieve the Universal Way of life, it is essential that one take no thought of the personal benefit that results from one's virtuous behavior. This is the way to fulfill one's own universal nature.

"Kind prince, one who is integrally virtuous does not sit back and enjoy the loftiness of his personal spiritual achievement while the world engages in bloodshed because of people's ignorant attachments to particular ideologies and theologies. One of integral, universal virtue is not interested in personal exaltation. He exposes the truth and shows the way for the evolution of all humanity. Any individual's spiritual achievement can never be considered great as long as the world is victimized by wars.

"Kind prince, those who brandish power are like small children playing with an enormous ax; they will inevitably bring about their own destruction. Undeveloped humanity can destroy itself through its own ignorance, and this is why one of universal virtue has something of great value to say and share with people. His purpose is not to share the excellence of his mind nor to display his great compassion. It is simply the natural responsibility of one who can see to tell a blind horseman on a blind horse that he is riding toward an abyss."

The prince asked, "Venerable Teacher, I have only a minor question. I think I understand, but I am not sure. You often speak of universal awareness as the awareness of wholeness, complete awareness and bondage-free awareness. Would you please explain this further to my limited mind?"

"Kind prince," replied the master, "awareness is the subtle movement of the mind. It is different than thought in that it can be reflective and light up your own mistakes as well as those of others. In general, awareness is conditioned by momentary reflections of things or symbols. It is something that can send your mind deep into further levels of understanding, thus your question is not a minor one but a great one. The integral truth of one universal life is achieved by the attainment of integral, universal awareness and whole enlightenment. These are key spiritual offerings to all who are willing to reach for them. They are one in matter of fact, although I have spoken of them as separate things so that my listeners can understand. One of universal awareness and whole enlightenment sees the physical world of the sun, moon and stars, which extends to the Silver River (the galaxy) and the Star Clouds (nebulae), as different parts of one's physical body. Highly evolved souls become the soul of the physical multi-universe. Depending on the development of the individual's mind and spirit, one can discover not only the great universal body but achieve true awareness and enlightenment of the soul and the reality of one universal life."

THIRTY

"Venerable Teacher, it is clear that if one person offers worldly treasure as alms to those in need while another person practices the Universal Way of life and expounds its truth to others, the blessings of the latter will be much greater than those of the former, for one who expounds the Universal Way is able to avoid the extreme of partialism."

The master replied by saying, "Kind prince, this kind of relative comparison may have some value, but the highest teaching is wordless because the subtle integral truth itself is unspeakable, unexplainable and unthinkable. One who tries to talk about it only deviates from it and makes it obscure. One who thinks about it loses it. All we can do, therefore, is show the way to the traveler; we cannot walk it for him. We can write the prescription, but we cannot drink the bitter herbal tea for him. All teachings are like medicine which is given to the sick according to the disease they have.

"There is no single word which can be held as the total truth, there is only the universal integral way of life. A universal being lives quietly, connecting himself with the wordless truth of life undividedly, selflessly and harmoniously. He does not connect himself with any social, religious or political position, but always chooses the truth in any situation."

"In this case, Venerable Teacher, is it correct to say that, according to the integral truth, those who offer alms to people in need and those who expound the Universal Way accumulate blessings equal to nothing?"

"Kind prince," replied the master, "the blessings are neither something nor nothing. Both the offering of alms and the expounding of the Universal Integral Way are manifestations of positive energy which will evoke a corresponding response from the universe.

"Kind prince, what do you think? Can beauty be put into words?"

"No, Venerable Teacher, true beauty speaks for itself."

"Tell me, kind prince, can perfection be put into words?"

"No, Venerable Teacher, true perfection speaks for itself."

"Kind prince, can the integral truth be put into words?"

"No, Venerable Teacher, it, too, speaks for itself."

"Kind prince, there are two kinds of disciples who follow the Universal Integral Way. One kind understands it intellectually and is able to speak about it well, while the other actually lives it with his whole being."

THIRTY-ONE

The master continued, "Kind prince, if someone thinks that the subtle cosmic body of the Universal One comes and goes, sits and lies down, then this individual has not understood what I am saying. Why? Because the subtle cosmic body comes and goes nowhere, yet is always everywhere. Although it is called the subtle cosmic body, its reality cannot be put into words. To be aware of being with the Universal One is like watching the reflection of the moon on the surface of a still lake. Actually, the moon is not in the lake, yet people speak of it so. If, by chance, clouds appear and cover the moon, people say it has departed from the lake, yet it has actually gone nowhere.

"The relationship between the universal soul and the individual soul is just like the relationship between the moon and the lake. Spiritual security is always present, but the clouds of the mind create the phenomena of apparent separation. The true nature of the universe is always self-existent, never failing to respond to an individual's straight and direct awareness. If an individual is aware enough, he realizes that the Universal One does not only come at the time of awareness. When one's mind is disturbed or confused, the Universal One seems to disappear, yet one's true nature has not departed. One creates the darkness which covers the light that is always available to freely support one's soul.

"It is the double vision of the mind which lead people to create mischief, agony, misery and tragedy. The source of all suffering is an individual's stubborn adherence to the establishment of self which separates him from his universal nature. It is not the Universal Way that chooses to be with one person and not another.

"There are no images which should be held onto and no blessings which should be sought. There is no single virtue on which one should focus, nor any special names one should revere. Thus, when one attains universal awareness he can directly rejoin his true nature, which is the subtle cosmic body of the Universal One."

THIRTY-TWO

"Kind prince, if someone could smash the universe into small bits, do you think there would be very many particles?"

"There would be very many indeed, Venerable Teacher, but only if they really existed individually. To the Universal One, the individual small particles would not be individual small particles; they are merely named so. The so-called worlds are but the conjoining of the individual small particles. To the Universal One, the occurrence of conjoining is not real but is merely called so."

"Kind prince, each small particle is an entire world in itself. The worlds are the conjoint movement of small particles. There is no real difference between small particles and the vast world, but they are differently named because of the relative concepts of small and vast. When the small particles gather, there is the world; when the world disperses, there are small particles. It is not accurate to say they are different. Neither is it accurate to say that the world is a heap of small particles with varied formations, nor that the small particles conjoin and gather as the world. One cannot be distinguished as being primary and the other as secondary because in reality there is no difference between the two.

"There are no grounds for believing that the movement of conjoining and dispersing is either with or without purpose. Nor are there any grounds for commenting on whether those movements are the mischief of blind, mechanical, physical nature or the wonderful creation of an artistic, universal mind. It is all the same when one has the insight to see the deep nature of things. It is different when one is bewildered by the diversified movements on the surface of reality. When people hold fast to their egos, they are bewildered by the question of whether it is the same thing or different, thus it is the ego which blinds people to the great equality of universal reality. The relative concepts of sameness and difference are merely manipulations of the mind and have nothing to do with reality. They preoccupy one with mere names and prevent the direct perception of reality.

"The world and the particles are not separate, isolated things. The particles could be gathered to become the world, and the world could be dispersed to become particles. One small particle contains the nature of the world, and the world contains the nature of each small particle; the nature of each is the same. Thus, although they are not one and the same, neither are they different. If one is attached to names, however, one can never achieve a clear, direct perception of the integral truth of all things.

"Kind prince, each small particle is a world of matter. At the same time it is a world of spirituality. It possesses both spirituality and materiality. Likewise, every event is a conjoint entity of many different elements. In reality, each conjoint entity is not an isolated, single event, but is only regarded and named as such. The apparently single event is a variation and segment of the great whole. The great whole is the combination of all single events. The single events contain the life experience of the whole. The great whole contains the life substance of the single events and vice versa. Thus, in reality, there is no discrimination between single events and the great whole; both are equal.

"Everything in the universe is equal. The great equality of reality comprises the subtle cosmic body of the Universal One. However, the direct perception of this Oneness is blocked by established mental concepts which separate us from the truth of universal being.

"Kind prince, ignore both the world and the particles, the single event and the conjoint mass. Embrace only the unnameable Oneness. You will find yourself and all good things there. What about the bad things? No bad things, no bad thoughts, and no extraneous thoughts can exist there."

THIRTY-THREE

The master continued, "Wise prince, the individual body is the cosmic body. This refers not only to humankind, but to all beings. The cosmic body is not separate from the individual body, nor is the individual body separate from the cosmic body.

"The small particle which I referred to before is associated with the individual body. When the world diversifies into small particles, it is like the cosmic body appearing as the individual body. Just as the small particles gather, comprising the vast world, the individual actualizes the cosmic body. The cosmic body must not be thought of as something separate from the whole, for it is whole itself and generates all individual bodies. Though small particles individually may not be the world, together they may comprise the body of the world. While the world may not be small particles, it could be traced back to the small particles.

"The cosmic body may be comprehended as the vast and profound universe, but it is not observable in physical terms. It is beyond reach, yet at the same time it is also within reach.

"The relationship between the world and the small particles is somewhat similar to the relationship between a flower and a mirror which reflects it. The mirror reflects the flower, and through this reflection the existence of the mirror may be perceived. But in the relationship between the small particles and the world, it cannot be decided which side is the reflection and which is being reflected. Both reflect each other; neither can be held as the substance.

"The relationship between the cosmic body and the individual body is something like the relationship between the moon and its reflection on a lake. One side seems to be the real thing and the other just its reflection, but even the moon is only reflecting the light of the sun, and the sun is not the final source either. There is nothing substantial which is final.

"When small particles take on some configuration, they may appear solid and fixed, however, they are neither solidly formed nor perpetually changing. It seems true that the world really exists in time and space, but it is merely a transient, conjoint event in this place and time. It also seems true that the individual body really exists in time and space, but it too is merely a transient, conjoint event in this place and time. Even the structure of time and space themselves is not real, but is only a conceptual creation. In the totality of truth, all things are not one and the same, but neither are they different. Their configuration as a conjoint entity does not last forever, but neither are they isolated and separate forever. To the Universal One, conjoint movement is only an illusion, as is dispersion, yet the mind labels them as distinct. Universal reality is always beyond any attempt of the mind to categorize or make distinctions about it."

THIRTY-FOUR

"Very well, kind prince," said the master. "What do you think? Can small particles gather together to become a soul?"

"Venerable Teacher, when a star exists, its light exists. When the star disappears, its light also disappears; the star's subtle energy, however, does not die away. It either remains in the subtle realm or transfers to those connected with it.

"Human life and all things in the universe begin in the subtle realm of the unmanifest and are then brought forth into the realm of the manifest where they assume physical form. A human being is certainly a gathering of small particles, and when one is alive, the vitality is there. When one passes away the vitality disperses, but not the subtle energy. The energy may remain in the subtle realm or be transferred to those who may connect with it according to the law of energy response.

"What I wish to know, Venerable Teacher, is how long the life force of a human being can last."

"Kind prince, the potency of a human being can last very long indeed. In one lifetime a person may be born into a family or race or society or nation that he once loved, while in another lifetime he will be born into a family or race or society or nation toward which he was hostile. The person may be born with a shape that was once attractive to him or with one which disgusted him. Emotional attachment such as love or hate is heavy, gross energy, and it is this kind of energy that influences how one forms one's new life and environment in response to what one has projected mentally, emotionally and physically."

THIRTY-FIVE

"Venerable Teacher," asked the prince, "when a person passes away, does his cognition pass with him in his future lives?"

"Kind prince, the basic function and ability of cognition continues its growth when a soul is reborn into the physical world, however, the content of cognition is generally not carried with the soul. This is especially true of those people who have spent many years in intellectual pursuits. Except for the deep experience of certain training that is strongly built and forged, knowledge is stripped away because the storage of such information is related to the brain cells rather than to basic patterns and deep instincts of life."

"Venerable Teacher, can intuitional ability be passed on from one lifetime to the next?"

"Kind prince, insight is not the content of knowledge. Because it is not of the realm of the intellect, it continues whenever and wherever the being exists."

"Venerable Teacher, can it be said that insight is immortal then?"

"Kind prince, it is the being which is immortal, and some of the ability. If a being develops his insight but does not achieve immortality, the insight will follow the same cycle of life, death and rebirth that the person follows. If the person achieves immortality, however, he will be an immortal being with pure insight."

THIRTY-SIX

"Venerable Teacher, is it possible for an individual to uplift himself to the immortal realm and enjoy pure freedom and perfect happiness?"

"Kind prince," replied the master, "it is possible. Undiscriminating virtue is the vehicle that transports one there; it expresses the highest energy of universal nature. It brings forth all lives and offers support to the development of all human beings. It is the conjoint energy of high spiritual beings who respond to all energy of the same subtle frequency as their own. The most powerful protection one can have from negative influences is the whole virtue of a natural life. This is the simple reality of the law of energy response. Kind and selfless beings lead a life attuned to the Universal Way. With whole virtue they eliminate the artificial boundaries between societies and the illusory boundary between life and death. In this way they become immortal."

"Venerable Teacher, do all immortal divine beings have insight?"

"Kind prince, it is not a question of whether they have insight into one particular thing or not, but whether a being has cultivated and developed the vision of wholeness before realizing an integral life of immortality. If a person learns only the technique of gathering energy in order to become immortal, but does not develop his entire being and complete vision, then his cultivation depends entirely on the information he is able to gather. Even if he is fortunate enough to learn the right way from a secret book or special instruction, he will probe in darkness and may succeed in becoming immortal only by grace. Most likely, he will meet with many kinds of trouble before he ever gets that far, unless his virtue is complete."

"Venerable Teacher, if one develops insight trough practicing a secret system of self-cultivation, can he become an immortal without any difficulties?"

"Kind prince, it is not that those with knowledge of a secret system of self-cultivation do not encounter the problems of life, but rather that they are thoroughly equipped to deal with them successfully. One should not think of difficult situations as being trouble, but rather as the unfolding of a virtuous life and its subtle laws."

"Venerable Teacher, I understand that one who is cultivating himself in order to evolve to the immortal realm must not try to hide in a corner and avoid the reality of life. He must face the reality of worldly life, for the reality of one's cultivation and development lies in learning to solve all possible difficulties through the unfoldment of one's complete vision which sees the integral truth."

"Kind prince, there can be no complete development for those who do not live a complete life. A complete life is the foundation for the attainment of immortality. If an individual's energy is distorted and imbalanced because of partial development, this contradicts the law of existence and disintegrates the person's being. The result is not only the loss of possible immortality, but the very dissolution of life itself."

THIRTY-SEVEN

"Venerable Teacher, is an individual responsible for whether his life is pleasant or unpleasant and for whether it has a happy or unhappy ending? Is he also responsible for the lives of others?"

"Kind prince, after one takes form as an individual entity, suffering and enjoyment continue throughout many lifetimes and even during the subtle intermission between lives. Actually, to suffer and enjoy seems to be the destiny of an individual, but its extent is determined by the way in which one subjectively forms one's energy, consciously and unconsciously.

"With regard to whether a person is responsible for the lives of others, it is not a question of responsibility, but of how one manifests one's energy.

"Kind prince, what do you think? Is the subtle stage of life the root of one's life, and is the visible stage the tree? Or is the invisible stage the tree and the active stage the root?"

"Venerable Teacher, I now understand that each stage of life is the root of the next stage, with each event as an element of the total event. This is the way one continuously forms one's life and destiny."

"Kind prince, to the Universal One there is no tree and no root. This means that there is no isolated, single event; all events are related. There is no tree, therefore, that is separate from its root, nor any root that is separate from the tree. Neither can it be separated from the soil, the climate and the natural environment. The integrity of the tree depends on the normalcy of nature and the mercy of mankind. This also holds true for the life of a human being."

"Venerable Teacher, what is the relationship between a soul and its physical life?"

"Kind prince, take this pine tree as an example. It has strong roots, a stout trunk, numerous branches, twigs, cones and needles, yet it started from a tiny seed. The original seed from that tree was formed from warmth, wind, water and earth; however, this combination alone does not make a tree. The most important components are the energy rays emanating from numerous sources. Even the energy of remote stars and the sun and moon. The spontaneous integration of all these ingredients nurtures the chance of a new life and brings beauty and intelligence to life.

"Kind prince, all plants, animals, races of people and many kinds of insects are images and symbols of the energy of various natural environments and are associated with the network of rays from different stars. The first invisible 'seeds' of energy bestowed on the earth originated from this network of energy rays. In one ancient ceremonial ritual, the integrally developed ones stated the great truth of life by saying, 'Heaven is our father and Earth is our mother. All living things are our brothers and sisters.' We must respect and be at peace with all the various forms of life, no matter how different they may appear."

THIRTY-EIGHT

"Venerable Teacher, I was told that the first being to appear in the world was called Pan-Kou. In the beginning, the universe was like a sealed stone drum and, after many years, the density inside of the drum began to change. From this stone was born Pan Kou who shaped the universe into Heaven and Earth and divided himself into many, many life beings. His name literally means 'big round drum.' Does this mean that the first human being and his descendants were shaped like drums, with no intelligent development, or that all human beings are merely like someone living in a drum, not knowing what goes on outside the drum?"

"Kind prince, when I was at my teacher's side I asked the very same question. My kind teacher sang a song to me in response. As well as I can recall it, I will sing it now to you:

The Song of Pan Kou

Old Pan Kou knows nothing about time
*   and nothing about space as well.*
His life is self-natured and self-sufficient.
He needs to ask for nothing outside of his own being.
The genesis of the world is the exercise of his mind.
When his mind starts to think, the world starts to move.
The world has never been made by any special design.
Neither has an end ever been put to it.
Old Pan Kou swings his ax and chisels rhythmically.
From it comes Heaven, but not as you think of it,
*   and Earth, but not as you see it.*
Everything is the way it naturally is.
Since the young gods who are the descendants
*   of Pan Kou follow only impulse,*
*   they make moves that disturb the world.*
The wise and old ones sit still
*   and watch the chess games of the foolish.*
All the changes in the world
*   are displayed upon the chess board.*
Victory and defeat are decided
*   by the subtle elements behind the moves.*
It can clearly be seen by the wise.
The wise who love their life and value
*   their words remain quiet and watch.*
If the foolish gods only knew it,
*   there is perfect originalness*
*   before any move is made.*
It is what offers beings the opportunity of life.
When an artificial move is made,
*   the subtle root begins to die.*
When peace is disturbed,
*   the vital energy passes.*

The kindness of Pan Kou
*   is expressed as harmonious nature.*
The further downfall of his descendants
*   causes the knowledge of the treasures*
*   that are hidden in nature to be lost.*
They look everywhere for it,
*   making wasteful, competitive moves.*
If any of them knew to look at the example
*   of old Pan Kou's life,*
*   could they live fully with the same divine,*
*   immortal nature of old Pan Kou?*
Old Pan Kou never made any unnatural moves.
The true path of divine life keeps moving with him.

If a person looks for the path outside himself,
*   he will find his shadow*
*   and depart from the true substance.*
The diverging paths of life multiply greatly
*   with each generation.*
The lost sheep cannot be found
*   because of so many side paths.*
Once divergence is eliminated,
*   all Heavens and Earths,*
*   all lost sheep² and old Pan Kou himself*
*   return to original oneness.*
The good and healthy world of endless life
*   starts generating again, without anyone's command.*

"Kind prince, to have knowledge is to create doubt, and to have doubt is to create the need for knowledge. Let it suffice to say that the named was born from the unnamed. The describable world comes from the indescribable Source. Before the good life is spoiled, let everything be its own truth, for the truth of one individual is the truth of the entire

---

²*A star, a group of stars, or a nebula.*

universe. Let everything be united with the truth of its own being.

"The totality of truth presents itself to you instantaneously every time you blink your eyes. It can dance on the tip of your eyelash. It stretches as far as the eye can see and fills as much as the mind can hold. It exists in every moment of time and every bit of space. Is there any instant which does not contain the truth of life? Is there any place which does not hold the truth of existence and non-existence? Take the example of the pine tree. Which inch of the living tree is not the truth? Which hour that the tree lives is not the truth? Are people not living trees?"

"Venerable Teacher, will people of future generations, during the Age of Confusion, be able to understand such truth?"

"Kind prince, in the future, in the Age of Confusion, people will create many obstacles to knowing the simple truth and hold fast to their own blindness and falsehoods. They will persuade others to follow them and will persecute unbelievers and even start wars against them.

"Kind prince, the one who searches for the truth loses it. The one who wishes to hold the truth causes it to slip away from him. Because one departs from his own nature to search for something external, he overlooks the truth of his own being. To be is to be true. The muchness and suchness of truth is included in this very second. If you miss the truth of this moment, a thousand galloping horses cannot catch up with it."

THIRTY-NINE

"Venerable Teacher, is there a great creator of the universe, and did this creator bring forth all things and beings?"

"Kind prince, there is creation, but it itself is uncreated. There is transformation, but it itself is not transformed. The uncreated is able to create and recreate, and the untransformed is able to transform and retransform. That which is created cannot help producing of itself, and the transformed cannot help transforming of itself. By this is meant that there is no time and space without the production or transformation of things of themselves. This is the exhibition of *yin* and *yang*, metaphorically expressed as the swing of old Pan Kou's ax. The untransformed goes to and fro. The range of what goes to and fro is unlimitable. The Universal Way has neither beginning nor end and is inexhaustible. As the Universal One says:

The subtle essence of the universe is eternal.
It is like an unfailing fountain of life
*   which flows forever in a vast and profound valley.*
It is called the Primal Female,
*   the Mysterious Origin.*
The operation of the opening and closing
*   of the Gate of Origin performs*
*   the Mystical Intercourse of the universe.*
This Mystical Intercourse brings forth all things
*   from the unseen sphere into the realm of the manifest.*
The Mystical Intercourse of yin and yang
*   is the root of universal life.*
The subtle, gentle movement of the interplay
*   between yin and yang never ceases.*
Its creativity and usefulness are boundless.

"Therefore, kind prince, that which creates things is itself uncreated, and that which transforms things is itself nontransformed. Creation, transformation, form, appearance, wisdom, energy, decline and cessation all take place by themselves within the universal subtle law. It is incorrect to say that any of these must be achieved through external effort.

"Kind prince, if one insists on the conditions under which things develop and searches for the causes thereof, such searching and insistence will never end until one comes to something that is unconditional. Then the principles of self-transformation will become clear.

"There are those who say that the semi-shadow penumbra is conditioned by the shadow, the shadow by the body and the body by the creator. However, the creator is uncreated and all forms materialize by themselves, just as the great *T'ai Chi* is 'self-so.' Throughout the entire realm of existence, one will see that there is nothing, not even the semi-shadow, that does not transform itself beyond the phenomenal world. Hence, everything creates itself through the integration of *yin* and *yang*, without the direction of any creator. Since all things create themselves, they are self-determined. This is the immortal model of the universe.

"Kind prince, there is not a single thing in the universe that has been accomplished. There is also not one thing that is unaccomplished. The 'accomplished' is called the phase of stillness and rigidity: the 'unaccomplished,' the phase of dynamics and flexibility. The still phenomenon is called *yin*, and the dynamic phenomenon is called *yang*. The *yang* is always pushing itself forward, looking for accomplishment, while the *yin* is always receptive to joining *yang* and continuing the process of accomplishment. The integration of *yin* and *yang* is called *T'ai Chi*.

"Everything that exists is an expression of *T'ai Chi*. Every small particle is a *T'ai Chi*. The vast universe is a *T'ai Chi*. A single event is a *T'ai Chi*. The gathering of small events or units is a *T'ai Chi*. The dispersing of the vast universe is a *T'ai Chi*. There is nothing beyond *T'ai Chi* or excluded from it. Thus, the individual body is a *T'ai Chi*. The cosmic body is also a *T'ai Chi*. *T'ai Chi* is the integral truth of the universe."

FORTY

"Venerable Teacher," said the prince, "now it is completely clear to me: the path of subtle integration of *yin* and *yang* operates behind all phenomena and penetrates even the smallest particles of substance. Substance is merely the condensation of energy; everything in the universe is an expression of the subtle path and universal law that permeates all time and space. Nothing can evade it. The subtle law is as natural and essential as breathing. Just as when people stop breathing they violate the normalcy of the body, when anything violates the subtle law, there is immediate disaster.

"There is a natural order of things which cannot be violated or dismissed. Food, for example, is eaten through the mouth not the nostrils and we see through our eyes not our ears. Everything has its natural function with which one cannot argue. Functions are many and varied, but they all serve nature.

"At first, one may be ignorant of the subtle path because one is aware of particular phenomena rather than the subtle connection between what he thinks and says and does and what appears in his universe. When a person becomes aware of this connection, he may begin to cultivate himself in order to align his life with the subtle order of universal life. As he develops, he gradually discovers that all things are subtly connected through the cosmic body, but at this stage cosmic law is still perceived as one thing and his own being as another. Often such a person feels troubled, because he thinks the subtle law confines him and that he is at its mercy. This is because he still entertains the notion of self and sees the subtle law as something external to himself. His desires fight his mind, his mind fights his spirit, and he is in a constant state of conflict and turmoil, both within himself and with the world around him. He may struggle throughout his whole lifetime. If, however, the struggle motivates him to further cultivate himself, to disperse his desires and cleanse the obscurity of his mind, it gradually dawns on him that he and the subtle path are one. There is no separation. He is not the isolated individual he thought himself to be. All divine, subtle beings, all enlightened beings are one with him. What happiness one experiences in that state of consciousness!

"Yet, in reality, there is nothing called happiness nor anything called unhappiness. The concepts of happiness and unhappiness are creations of the dualistic mind; neither of them exists in the integral realm. When one is in the integral realm, Heaven and Earth and the myriad things are like one's own fingers. The physical universe is like the palm of one's hand. When all truth is manifest within oneself, there is a profound serenity that no one else can reach. Only the one who tastes it knows it.

"There is no one who can pass judgement on another person. Each individual is the master of his own life and death, the master of mortality and eternal life. What he does is what he is. This is the spiritual truth. Profound truth is always simple, yet the universal being does not call it either simple or profound."

FORTY-ONE

"Kind prince, if someone says the Universal One denies the reality of self and others or of life and death, what do you think?   Does this person understand what the Universal One says?"

"No, Venerable Teacher, the person does not understand. The Universal One says that to affirm the notions of self and others, life and death, is equal to denying these notions, for both are merely points of view, definable concepts which can be comprehended by the mind through images and speech. All relative mental creations and conditions of life, whether ideological, pragmatic, or theological, are merely dreams, delusions, bubbles, and shadows which last no longer than the early morning dew or summer lightning in the sky. All manipulations of the mind are totally futile. The relative mind creates only conflict, both within itself and with others. One notion fights another notion; one time fights another time; life becomes full of contradiction, misery and tragedy."

The master said, "Kind prince, a universal being does nothing to fragment his mind. He dissolves all his delusions with his integral universal awareness. The span of a human life is as quick as a dream or a bubble or a shadow and as fleeting as the morning dew or summer lightning in the sky. However, this is no reason to be irresponsible and eschew an honest life. Why so? The short is just as valuable as the long. Time is not a matter of accumulation."

FORTY-TWO

"Kind prince, what do you think? Are the world of ideas and the real world one and the same or are they two different worlds?"

"Venerable Teacher," replied the prince, "there is no such thing as a world of ideas. The world of ideology is merely a distorted reflection of the mind. It is a mental delusion, a deviation from the real world. When one keeps one's mind simple, undistracted, and unconditioned, the double vision of the mind is soon dissolved. Then one can see the one moon again. There is no mystery about this."

"Kind prince," continued the master, "there is nothing in the realm of ideas that is absolute and because of this, all efforts to form ideologies are ultimately futile. Only by dissolving the mind can one connect with the one great universal life.

"In reality, everything is integral, because the Universal Integral Way is the only way that exists. The confrontational nature of duality is merely an illusory product of the mind. In order to perceive the integral reality of the universe, it is necessary to transcend the mental process of separation and fragmentation. For one who has transcended the divergence of duality, there is only the integral way of life. Because the integral way of life exists, it is possible to transcend the dualistic mind.

"The integral or universal mind knows that there is no self, that everything is One-Self; thus it understands that if one does something outwardly to others, one in fact has done it inwardly to oneself. Every being is the center of his own universe, his own conjoint reality, and everything

about him is one element which composes his conjoint
world."

FORTY-THREE

"**K**ind prince, there is great power in an integrated and
sincere mind. By keeping their minds whole and
untouched, the ancient sages evolved profound mental and
spiritual abilities. They understood that intellectual development by itself fragments the mind and can lead a person
far from the true nature of life. In the future, humanity will
overemphasize the intellectual element of the mind. Instead
of recognizing the wholeness of life, people will perceive life
as having a worldly aspect and a spiritual aspect that are
separate and unrelated to each other. People will also, lose
themselves in isolated fragments of conceptual information
and become the victims rather than the masters of their
knowledge.

"The remedy for people of the future age of great
confusion lies in the ancient knowledge of the integral way
of life that has been passed down from generation to
generation. The holistic way of life practiced by the ancient
sages incorporated body, mind and spirit as a whole in all
activities. Their clothing, diet and dwellings were in accord
with nature. They relied on their limbs for transportation.
Their education was broad and comprehensive; it did not
emphasize one element of their being while neglecting the
others. They did not seek out special activities for recreation;
their work and recreation were one and the same. Their
forms of exercise developed not only the body, but the mind
and spirit as well through the harmonization of their internal
energies. Their music functioned as a bridge of communica-
tion between mind and spirit and was not just an emotional
release. Their leaders were chosen because they were
outstanding models of virtue, not for their financial or
military capabilities. Philosophy, science and spiritual practice were incorporated as one whole.

"Kind prince, an individual's true growth occurs in the process of solving the problems of life. All difficulties can be resolved through following the holistic, integral way of life."

The prince replied, "Venerable Teacher, how can people in the future era of confusion deal with their greatly troubled times?"

"Kind prince, the people of the future should not blindly accept the new nor blindly reject the old. Things that were developed long ago may still have great value if they have been proven safe and effective by the test of time. The new inventions that will appear may seem to be short cuts, but things of temporal convenience will bring hidden troubles later. Future generations will need to reevaluate all old and new discoveries and inventions to insure that they are useful and healthy, according to the standards of a holistic way of life."

"Venerable Teacher, how does one recognize the Universal Integral Way?"

"Kind prince, one recognizes the Universal Way and reaches the highest level of personal spiritual development through the effort of searching and the continual process of refinement. Because one's own developed spiritual capability is the better pilot of one's life boat, some may call this the Universal Way, yet the Universal Way is not a discovery or established doctrine. Never be so childish as to think that one may concentrate on spiritual cultivation and moral discipline without making oneself virtuously useful by serving others. This kind of attitude is either a psychological illness or a childish game that trades religious devotion for psychological protection and transient emotional blessings."

FORTY-FOUR

"Kind prince," said the master, "those who are motivated to attain awareness of the universal truth should follow the way discussed in this sacred record in order to perceive, to know and to understand both the internal and the external. They should not be fooled by the false images of the mind. Attachment to the false images of the mind is the greatest obstacle to reaching awareness of the integral truth of the universe.

"Kind prince, to believe in the reality of images is equal to believing in the unreality of images. Both are mere concepts which separate one from direct intuitional contact with the integral truth. To know the truth is to know nothing, yet when one knows the truth, there is nothing one is not aware of.

"To have whole vision is to have no vision of anything in particular, yet there is nothing which can escape one's discernment. People who are unenlightened have not yet reached the universal truth, for they cannot direct their mental energy to flow in the right channel. Instead, they adhere to totally false, rigidly formed belief systems that are composed of concepts derived from their limited sensory organs. This distorted information is stored and arranged by the memory and judgement systems. Thus, the more one knows and understands, the more dimness and confusion are created. One is continually bewildered by what one knows and sees. If, by chance, one manages to avoid falling into the pitfall of the content of what one knows and sees, one invariably becomes trapped in the mechanics of how one knows and sees. If one is not confused by the appearance of what one sees, then one can be fooled by what enables one to see. The mind clings to the false images it creates. All of this conditioning builds up layer upon layer of conceptual filters through which one then looks at the world. Thus, not only is one's perception of the world distorted by the interposition of these false images, but one's very being becomes distorted. This adds further hindrance to reaching the universal truth.

"Kind prince, this is why it only aggravates the situation further to do anything to eliminate the vexation of the mind. In the process of working to eliminate mental vexation, more trouble and further separation are created. This prevents one from getting in touch with one's true being and from moving forward toward the integral reality of the universe. The

movement created by the attempt to eliminate mental
vexation, such as turning to religion for help or escape, is just
another deviation from the correct channel in which one's
mental energy should flow. If, at this moment, one does not
become attached to what one sees and knows, one can
uncover one's true insight and thereby see through the
illusory situations of life. Actually, attachment is the separation from the wholeness of truth. Theological promises, the
appearance of life and death, and all human activities are
fruitless compared to the universal truth. When one dissolves the illusion of separation from the source of the
Universal Mind, one restores one's own original, pure mind.
It is the accumulation of dust and dirt, gathered while living
in the world, that prevents one from truly experiencing the
fullness of life. Once the dust and dirt are cleansed away,
one suddenly becomes brilliantly illuminated with the
awareness of integral unity. It is not by creation or design
that one can enjoy awareness of oneness with the subtle
cosmic body, but only through the direct experience of the
Universal Way of life. Nor can one experience the Universal
Way of life by fastening oneself to anything the mind creates,
but only by following the Universal Integral Way can one see
and know correctly. Clarity and enlightenment are brought
about without one's having to move an inch, for the integral
truth is always found within one's own true nature."

FORTY-FIVE

The master continued his instruction. "Because the mind
is the central aspect of a human being, the rectification
of the mind in turn rectifies all of one's life activities so that
they flow in ne appropriate channel. The Universal Way of
life does not entail adding something to oneself; it depends
on decreasing something. One eliminates the *yin* elements
of one's life while nurturing and developing the *yang*
elements. The following is a guideline for all life in the

relative realm:

Eliminate the habitual, clinging tendency of consciousness and instead keep the mind detached and whole.

Eliminate all illusions and delusions and instead maintain true awareness.

Eliminate scattered and dissipating mental activities and concentrate instead on the purity of the unconditioned mind.

Eliminate all mental obscurity, and instead embrace crystal clarity.

Eliminate confused dreams and daydreams in order to protect and refine one's inner vision.

Eliminate disturbed emotion in order to return to serenity.

"Kind prince, in reality there is nothing to eliminate and nothing to establish. People deviate from their true nature and thus feel the need to do something to rectify their deviation, yet the more they do the farther they stray from their true nature. When one worships an idol or an image or an idea, it is like trying to wash water or creating a new head to put on top of the head one already has. Such activities merely add to people's restlessness. When people stop such restless activity, their integrity is spontaneously there. The solution lies in non-doing."

FORTY-SIX

"Venerable Teacher," began the wise prince, "I now understand that all ideas, thoughts, knowledge, and emotional reactions are totally empty. There is not one single thing in life that can be held as the final and complete truth. One should not be preoccupied with the trivialities of life, therefore, but should dedicate oneself to the immutable truth of Universal Oneness."

"Kind prince, the Unnameable gives birth to One: a single phenomenon. The One gives birth to Two: the single phenomenon divides itself in two. The Two give birth to

Three, for there must be something between every polarity. And the Three give birth to myriad things. All things are embodied by *yin* and embrace *yang* as their essential core.

"The Five Subtle Phases are the parallel evolutionary movement of all phenomena. Everything in the universe can be categorized according to the Eight Great Manifestations.

"Kind prince, if anyone holds the One, he must neglect the Two. If he holds the Two, he must neglect the Three. If he holds the Three, he must neglect the myriad things. Each stage of development is the reality of the universe, yet one cannot hold one stage as the complete reality. Therefore, kind prince, ignore the One, the Two, the Three and the myriad things. Do not take a part as the whole, because a part is not the whole. Do not take the whole as the whole, because any part is the whole."

"Venerable Teacher, I understand that I should have no attachment to anything, either the absolute or the relative, either the One or the myriad things."

"Kind prince, holding 'no attachment' as truth is still a deviation from the truth. When one rejects one side to hold another, one is still in the relative realm. One's mind should be like a smooth pearl rolling on a very even disc; it should move without the slightest interruption or stagnation. Moving is normal, stagnation is sickness."

"Venerable Teacher, I shall be very glad when I reach the stage where my mind is as refined as a pearl and my life experience is like an even disc."

"Kind prince, get rid of the images of the pearl and the disc, for they are not real. When one appears, the other appears, and when one disappears, the other also disappears. What can be called the mind? What can be called the experience? There is nothing which can be called the 'pearl-like mind' or 'disc-like experience'; they are merely conditions. So-called pain and happiness are merely conditions as well, and if one dissolves one's ego, what can be called pain and what misfortune? What can be called happiness and what good fortune?

"Kind prince, when one establishes the One, then there must be Two. When Two are established, there must be

Three. When Three have been established, there must be myriad things and then you have all kinds of divergence and diversity. Therefore, kind prince, to dissolve the One is to dissolve the myriad things. The way to unite the diversity is not to search for unity. Forget about searching for Oneness; do not bother to harmonize anything. The universe is already harmonious. Followers of religion are always looking for inner peace, but they lose their inner peace in searching for it."

"Venerable Teacher, I deeply appreciate your profound teaching on spiritual self-evolution. I completely comprehend that this great teaching is of the mental sphere, yet I cannot ignore the reality of life, of nature and of the universe."

"Kind prince, the total subtle reality is unnameable, indescribable and unthinkable, however, this does not mean that it cannot be known. It is merely unknowable to the conceptual mind; it is beyond thinking and language. The innate faculties of intuition and insight cannot be put into nameable, describable terms. Intuition knows the whole; intellect knows only fragments. People tend to develop only one aspect of the mind; this is hazardous and causes imbalance. Stop chiseling away the wholeness of the mind. All truth is there. All happiness in life is there."

"Venerable Teacher, I will cultivate wholeness of mind and develop my intuition and insight as the ultimate cultivation."

"Kind prince, there is no need to develop anything. Take away the weeds and the crop will grow naturally by itself. The purpose of self-cultivation is natural self-transformation. You do not need to weed out the hindrances; to do so is to create more hindrances. All that is necessary is to maintain serenity, yet serenity is not the final goal.

"All the principles of nature are contained within the wholeness of an individual's vision. These principles are the Subtle Path, the polarizing movement between the unmanifest and the manifest, the cyclic pattern of all changes, the Five Subtle Phases as the self-balancing function of nature, and the Eight Great Manifestations as the general categories of all phenomena. The intuitional vision of an individual does not exclude nature. One uses nature to intuit nature; one uses nature to restore and evolve nature. All truth is contained in *T'ai Chi*, and *T'ai Chi* is everything; there is nothing beyond it. The truth of cultivating the mind is to balance its polarities. The same truth also applies to the cultivation of the body and spirit. Learning this way, people will be able to achieve world peace.

"The secret of immortal cultivation and the harmonious universe is expressed in the *T'ai Chi* symbol ☯ . Even so-called self-nature cannot hold onto it. Everything takes something from something else. The basic structure of the universe that is generally recognized as time and space is not something solid. Time and space can change and dissolve, but the existence of a being or thing does not rely on the framework of time and space. Time and space have no self-nature. They are only accessories of an event, a thing or a being. Non-being does not mean that something does not really exist, but that it exists beyond the senses, time and space. Supernatural beings extend their life force freely to the lives of form and no-form and at the same time keep themselves unformed and supernatural. Is the supernatural something separate from the reality of nature? Wise prince, these two realities can be discussed separately, but both sides belong to the same substance of the great, one universal life. The subtle law of universal life emphasizes neither the natural nor the supernatural. In the process of human evolution, the universal truth is reached by one who is whole and who is not entrapped by natural or supernatural phenomena."

FORTY-SEVEN

"Kind prince, the confrontational nature of dualistic worldly life is so unhealthy; the way of misleading religions is distorted; the way of materialism is cruel; the way of blind spiritualization is unreal. Chanting is not more holy than the murmuring of a stream. Counting one's prayer's beads is not more sacred than normal breathing. Colorful religious robes are not more spiritual than plain civilian clothes. Therefore, relying on these superficial trappings of spiritual life will get one nowhere. The only way to attain the absolute state of being is through embracing absolute Oneness and leading a selfless life. By anonymously contributing to other's lives one may burnish the brightness of one's soul and radiate virtue to the world. Imbalance may be created by overdeveloping the physical or mental aspects of one's being. Be calm, happy and content with your own being, and live only according to your true nature.

"Kind prince, it is impossible to escape the destiny you have formed by your past actions. There is hope, however, for evolving and transforming one's being. Those who have all-encompassing, universal awareness are able to take responsibility for their lives and for their environment. They radiate a healthy influence to others and illuminate the world's darkness. Their absolute virtue becomes a sanctuary, not only for themselves, but for all beings. Virtue is the only true power of life. Those on the Universal Integral Way are resolutely dedicated to their own evolution and also to the evolution of all beings. Their lives are a process of self-refinement and self-transcendence. They are truly an extension of the Universal One."

FORTY-EIGHT

"Venerable Teacher," said the prince, "I now understand that there are two approaches to true spiritual cultivation. One is the affirmative approach which accepts and includes everything with a positive attitude. From an ethical point of view, it means extending universal virtue to all, regardless of any external condition. This is different from the relative, affirmative attitude that is expounded by religions and which includes some things or people and excludes others. According to the Universal Way, the affirmative approach excludes nothing.

"The other approach to spiritual cultivation involves the denial of all things external to one's own true nature. This includes the denial of all creations, all individuality, and all conditions. Only by denying these things can you unveil and unfold layer after layer of illusion. Finally, after all the layers have been peeled away, one comes to see the integral, universal truth.

"This may seem paradoxical, but the attitudes of affirmation and denial amount to the same thing. We accept all and deny all at the same time. If you deny all that is external to your true nature, you eliminate all mental entanglement and contamination and thereby raise your spirit and achieve crystal clarity. But the same thing happens by accepting all things without any partiality toward one particular thing. Both aspects are equally important, like the right and the left hands. In this way, *yin* and *yang* assist each other in order to transcend duality and achieve integral awareness.

"All of a person's viewpoints, concepts about life and religious convictions are a manifestation of his energy. If one's mind is strongly conditioned, it is as if one measures everything with a crooked ruler; he can never measure anything accurately. If one's aim, however, is to know the truth, then one must straighten and refine one's measuring instrument, for if the instrument is faulty, one cannot perceive reality precisely.

"When the nervous system of a human being is restored and refined, one becomes calm and objective. One can then see clearly and discover that although there is diversity in the universe, there is unity behind that diversity. One may intellectually learn, understand and accept the unity of the universe, but this is very different from arriving at the unity through personal spiritual purification. Struggling to achieve unity is not as natural as the spontaneous experience of and participation in unity itself. One cannot perceive the unity of the universe in terms of subject and object and still call it unity."

"Kind prince," said the master, "to the Universal One there is nothing to call unity and nothing to call diversity. There is nothing to call subject and nothing to call object. These are merely labels created by the dualistic mind."

FORTY-NINE

"Venerable Teacher, I am now deeply aware that to know or to think about something is much different than actually aligning oneself with the reality of being and doing it. To have a quick mind or tongue is not equal to real achievement. A person may think he is a good rider, but once he takes up the horse's reins, it takes time and practice in order to ride well. To talk and think about the Universal Integral Way is merely talking and thinking, which do not go beyond the relative realm; to a universal being, talking and thinking are irrelevant. The Universal Way is not just a matter of speaking wisdom, but one of continual practice in order to reach a universal realization. If one hopes to align oneself with it, one must practice it. If one does not practice it, one will never reach it. Although it takes years of practice to become one with the Universal Way, it takes but an instant to realize it."

"Kind prince," said the master, "just relax your body and quiet your senses. Forget that you are one among many. Undo the mind and allow it to return to its virgin purity. Loosen the spirits within you. Thus all things return to their root, and because there is no separation between them and their source, their return goes unrecognized. To know of the return is to depart from it. Do not be curious about its name and do not be in awe of its forms. Then the truth will present itself to you naturally of itself and you will join in oneness with deep and boundless reality. This is what it means to be a Universal One."

FIFTY

"Kind prince," continued the master, "one is just what one does. Behavior which is motivated by any kind of external pressure or internal impulse is not the straight expression of one's true nature. The only genuine behavior is that which is a direct expression of one's true, virtuous nature. When all of one's behavior is an extension of one's true nature, one may be called a natural universal being.

"Natural universal beings are the immortals of the universe. They never violate their true nature and thus are able to endure eternally. They are not like mortal beings who follow what is variable instead of what is invariable.

"Kind prince, what do you think? Should a person expend all of his vitality in order to actively accumulate more material things than he could possibly use in a life time? Should he do all kinds of good deeds in order to gather blessings in the next life? Or should he cultivate himself so that he may live in the spiritual realm? How much regard should he pay to the practical aspects of life?"

The prince humbly bowed to the master and said, "Venerable Teacher, according to the integral model you have established for all beings to follow, it is clear that one should live wholly and virtuously, following the Universal Way of life and making no discrimination between what is spiritual and what is mundane, what is present, past or future; ignoring all relative concepts, one should embrace only the immutable Oneness."

FIFTY-ONE

The master continued, "Kind prince, when one attains awareness of the subtle universal truth, one is able to comprehend all aspects of one's life. To realize the constancy and steadiness in your life is to realize the deep nature of the universe. This realization is not dependent on any transitory internal or external condition, rather it is an expression of one's own immutable spiritual nature. The only way to attain the Universal Way is to maintain the integral virtues of constancy, steadiness and simplicity in one's daily life.

"There are four cardinal virtues which assist one in achieving this goal. The first is unconditional natural piety. Natural piety means love and respect for one's being, both the internal aspects and the external manifestations. Unconditional natural piety is very different from the artificial, blind piety advocated by religions; it is a state of profound reverence toward natural life. People of later generations will need to restore this natural reverence which is arrived at through the rejection of all false images and concepts. When one's mind has been liberated from its bondage to illusion, one is spontaneously aware of the true sacredness of one's life in the universe. It is no longer necessary to create an external belief as the object of one's reverence, for one's own being and everything in one's environment are seen as divine in and of themselves.

"The second virtue is natural sincerity. To be naturally sincere means to be genuine, earnest, honest and whole-hearted. To be naturally sincere also means being free of all self-deception. To have no self-deception means to embrace the divine nature of life. Universal virtue among natural people is the integral nature of the universe. To be naturally sincere means to keep one's mind whole, unfragmented and centered. The distorted mind always suffers because it constantly creates separation and dichotomy, preventing real peace within. Keeping one's mind whole and at ease will not only assure inner peace so that one may transcend all transient trivialities, but it also reconnects one with the deep and constant nature of the universe.

"The third virtue is gentleness. When one is rough, one tends to be aggressive, inconsiderate and unkind to others. This behavior inevitably rebounds on oneself. When one is rough, one is also insensitive to the subtle truth of the universe. Roughness can lead to the destruction of one's connection with the spiritual realms, for the level of gentleness of one's being is the level of refinement of one's soul, and the more gentle and subtle one's energy, the closer one is to union with the subtle truth of the universe.

"The fourth virtue is being naturally supportive. This means that one does not set his mind to do only what he likes all the time, but in his spare time he helps others for positive purposes. To be a spiritual teacher or worker is to achieve oneself by serving others without reservation. Such virtue may take many years to develop through cultivating a skill or talent or wealth to a point where one can afford to serve without expecting anything big in return. Through serving others, one can find dignity and the true meaning of life.

"These four virtues are not an external standard or dogma, but attributes of one's true nature which is referred to as *Chen* or natural sincerity. These four virtues can give birth to all other virtues, the greatest of which are: *Jen* or impersonal love for all living things; *I* (pronounced eee) or propriety, rectitude and faithfulness in expressing natural friendliness; *Li* or moderation, self-restraint and non-aggression; *Tse* or wisdom; and *Sheng* or being reliable and trustworthy.

"All virtues lead to true blessings. The five greatest blessings are: *Fuh* or happiness that makes no demands; *Su* or longevity that does not make things short; *Kang* or health that is free from abuse; *Ning* or peace that is not self-disturbing or disturbing to others; and *Fui* or wealth that does not come about through scheming. Virtue is the mother of all blessings, for it not only brings forth blessings but also protects them.

"A universal being's positive attitude toward life is based on his correct awareness. He lives every moment of his life with virtue, thus every moment of his life is rightly accomplished. Living in this manner, one is free from any regret. The lives of those who achieve awareness of the integral oneness of the universe are models of virtue for the entire world."

FIFTY-TWO

"Venerable Teacher, I have been taught that a mind which is free of preconception is an empty mind. I understand that to practice empty mindedness does not mean suspending all thought, but rather keeping one's mind as clear as a cloudless sky. In this case, should one practice positive and creative thinking?"

"Kind prince, one should frequently empty one's mind by clearing away all confusion, disorder and dichotomy. This cleansing process is similar to using a basin full of water to wash a baby. After the baby is washed, the dirty water should be discarded, yet one should not discard the baby with the bath water. The individual who practices the cessation of thought in order to become a super-being is like one who discards the baby with the bath water. It is incorrect to practice empty mindedness without reaching whole-mindedness as a positive virtue of life."

"Venerable Teacher, should one spend all one's time and energy in quiet sitting meditation in order to remain above all worldly conditions and maintain empty mindedness?"

"Kind prince, one who spends all of his time and energy in quiet sitting meditation for this purpose is only fixing his mind in a certain, narrow way. This is not empty minded-ness, but only narrow mindedness. Such practice does not lead one anywhere, much less to become an integrally virtuous being.

"The practice of whole-mindedness, you see, is not the practice of stiffness. What is stiff belongs in the company of the dead, whereas what is supple belongs in the company of the living. The mindshould be like water that is always flowing smoothly. One should not designate a specific time or place in which to practice empty mindedness, but should practice mental unassertiveness in all aspects of life, the essential as well as the trivial."

The prince replied, "Venerable Teacher, should one intentionally and completely avoid all worldly troubles and activities for the purpose of practicing simplicity and keeping the mind clear?"

"Kind prince, if there were no worldly troubles and activities, how could one practice simplicity? Simplicity is the key to handling the troubles and activities of daily life. It is the deep reality of all natural and human matters, while the manifold forms are the events. Looking to the single essence to govern events is the meaning of simplicity in the practical sense."

"Venerable Teacher," asked the prince, "how should one practice integral virtue in daily life?"

"Kind prince, to have such universal virtue is to have unchangeable virtue. In daily life, one should fulfill one's obligations in the five great relationships. As a parent, one should love one's children. As a son or daughter, one should abide by one's parents deep wish for one to live a decent, healthy life. As a subordinate, one should carry out one's positive duty unfailingly with a sense of cooperation and teamwork. As a superior, one should assume full responsibility without blaming one's subordinates as an excuse. As a brother or sister, one should extend love and help to the younger ones, and the younger ones should do the same for the older ones. As a friend, one should be faithful. As a husband or wife, one should devotedly care for one's mate. In general, one should carry out any work that comes to one with righteousness. One should be concerned with making one's best contribution rather than seeking unrightful promotion and personal profit. One should practice steadfast and indiscriminative virtue without demanding others to do the same in return. These mental attitudes are the manifestation of such virtue."

"Venerable Teacher, what are the characteristics of one who is spiritually mature?"

"Kind prince, one who is spiritually mature is not a follower of dualistic religion. Most of the world's people worship the offspring, while one who is spiritually mature embraces the Source and never becomes the slave of any social or religious movement. He considers the world his family and accepts all people as his brothers and sisters. He offers his service to all and asks no recompense. He has broken through all perceptual obstructions and can see through all the diverse names which create discrimination and hostility, yet he respects natural variety and differences and treats all things as equal. He guards his life and the lives of others from negative destruction and does not foster unhealthy prosperity. He knows all the tricks of human beings, yet practices steadfast virtue. He has achieved awareness of the totality of truth, yet he maintains a simple, matter-of-fact manner. He may achieve supernatural abilities, yet he leads a plain life. He will be at the height of human spiritual achievement, yet he remains indistinguishable form ordinary people."

The prince then said, "Venerable Teacher, can one be complete if one practices universal heartedness and universal mindedness without learning the holistic, Universal Integral Way of life?"

"Kind prince, universal heartedness and universal mindedness are the Universal Way of life. There is only one Universal Way, but from different perspectives it is given different names."

"Venerable Teacher, I will practice the Universal Way of life with great joy and pass it on to all spiritual descendants so that it will be preserved generation after generation."

"Kind prince, the one who practices the Universal Integral Way shall be greatly blessed."

FIFTY-THREE

"Venerable Teacher, the instruction you have transmitted to us is rare and supreme guidance from the highest realm. You have led us to the Universal Way and taught us how to realize our own complete virtue. Your disciples, however, still dwell in the relative realm and are subject to the forces of *yin* and *yang* and the five subtle phases of energy. Would you teach us how we may use these forces to serve others and develop ourselves?"

"Kind prince," replied the master, "a person may learn to be completely virtuous, but if he is unable to serve others, or if his usefulness is limited by the fact that he himself needs help, then he cannot be said to be completely virtuous. A truly virtuous person cannot be indifferent to the troubled world in which he lives and must develop skills and methods by which to help himself and others. It is essential to understand that the truth of wholeness has two main attributes: substance and function. The substance is called *Ti*, the body or prime principle. The function is called *Yun* or usefulness. Together they are a complete *T'ai Chi* and serve as the two wings which can carry one to the integral realm. When this principle is applied to *yin* and *yang*, *yin* may be considered as the substance and yang the function, or vice versa. *Ti* and *Yun* are mutually dependent; in the deepest sense, substance is function and function is substance.

"During the three ancient generations of Fu Hsi, Sheng Nung and Huang Ti (the period of history prior to 3,000 B.C.E.), people did not need to do anything in order to be sages. They practiced 'non-partial doingness and minded-ness' and were naturally wise. Later, after this era had passed, people began to deviate from the integrity and virtue of originalness and it became necessary for them to practice self-cultivation in order to restore their wholeness and originalness. This restoration is referred to as the attainment of self-awareness. It corresponds with *Ti*, the substance of the Way, which enables people to reach the divine origin of non-making. In order to complete the *T'ai Chi*, however, it is necessary for those who have attained *Ti* to also extend *Yun*, the function and realization of the Way. This may happen through any constructive profession, business or activity. Only one who embodies both *Ti* and *Yun* can be called a man or woman of the Way.

"The interdependence of *Ti* and *Yun* is illustrated in the following story. A blind man and a lame man shared the same dwelling, and one day a cinder flew out of the fireplace. Within a short time the entire house was in flames.

Each man tried separately to escape, but neither could get out of the house. Finally the blind man said to the lame man, 'You have eyes and I have legs. If you climb on my back, you can direct me to the door.' In a few moments they were safely outside."

"Venerable Teacher," said the prince, "it is my sincere intention to become the embodiment of both *Ti* and *Yun* by cultivating crystal-clear awareness of the universal truth and extending unconditional virtue to the world."

FIFTY-FOUR

"Kind prince, your sincerity has moved me to reveal to you the tool which will enable you to realize your virtuous being. There are several categories of holistic subtle sciences which are vehicles for serving others and assisting one's own spiritual evolution. Within each category are hundreds of thousands of details which may be learned. It is not necessary to know all of them in order to reach the integral realm, however, one may make good use of them in one's life and for the benefit of others.

"Some of these holistic arts and sciences, which are actually systems of integral knowledge, were discovered through the spiritual unfolding of highly evolved beings who lived on earth during very ancient times. Others were developed through the power of intuition and the ability to link one's mind with the Universal Mind. Generation after generation, these methods have been passed down from highly evolved beings to virtuous individuals who are in the process of spiritual evolution to assist them in developing their spirit and intuition. If an individual does not develop his spirit and intuition, it is impossible to make full use of these techniques and this information to evolve to his fullest potential.

"This profound guidance is transmitted by a teacher of this esoteric tradition according to the disciple's personal needs and his or her potential for development. Since very

ancient times, it has been strictly prohibited to teach some
of the mystical knowledge and methods to the unvirtuous.
For this reason, those who have achieved a certain level of
development may discover, study and research these methods by themselves as evidence of their spiritual unfolding.
Those methods and subjects which are most practical should
be developed and disseminated to the general public. All of
the valuable, ancient methods should be preserved, protect-
ed and continually developed by people of high virtue in
future generations. Those who, because of intellectual
prejudice, disregard this wisdom will cause the setback of
human cultural development and spiritual evolution. This
will mark the beginning of humanity's great difficulty.

"Kind prince, those who guide themselves and others
with clear awareness illuminate the darkness of the world."

FIFTY-FIVE

The master then continued, "Kind prince, the holistic or
integral system of knowledge of the ancient sages is an
integration of science, art and personal spiritual development. The practice of these methods employs the laws of
nature and the subtle realm and involves the participation of
body, mind and spirit as an integral whole.

"I will mention a few of the subjects that comprise this
system. For instance, there are:

1) The holistic system of healing, referred to as *Yi Yau*.
Yi means healing, while *Yau* means seeking, preparing and
using medicinal materials. This science is a complete system
of diagnosis, acupuncture, herbology, therapeutic diet and
other healing techniques. The ancient developed ones, with
their developed mental and spiritual faculties, discovered
the relationship between nature and the human body which
enabled them to utilize medicinal plants. They were also
able to recognize certain points on the surface of the body
which are connected to the internal organs and specific

body systems and which become tender when a person is ill. When the illness goes away so does the tenderness. They developed advanced techniques of manipulating these points to influence the internal organs and systems. Through their deep insight, the ancient sages also discovered that diagnosis could be made by observing a person's aura, his eyes and ears, tongue, pulse waves, voice and movement as well as the specific symptoms of disease. The ability to correctly diagnose depends on the healer's personal achievement through training, spiritual self-cultivation and intuitional error-free response.

2) The holistic system of how to live a natural, healthy life. Systems of healing are only necessary when people become sick. The knowledge of healthy living is more important and was thus the core of cultural development in ancient China before social competition brought about the downfall of society.

Natural energy has cycles. Likewise, there are natural stages or cycles of human life. The importance of harmony between people and nature was fully recognized by the ancient wise ones, and the natural culture that they helped develop contained abundant knowledge in the art of human life.

3) The art of natural living led to the art of longevity, which includes breathing techniques, physical energy conducting exercises, important energy points of the body, diet and the use of herbal supplements, the spiritual practice of internal peace, and many other useful methods.

4) Even with all of these good methods, one cannot neglect the spiritual art for self-regulation, especially for the purpose of becoming attuned to the cycles of universal energy rotation through avoiding or accepting specific energy rays in daily life, referred to as *Shu-Ser* or Self-Cultivation and Life Discipline. This facilitates the complete spiritualization of one's being.

5) To know specific days of the solar cycle for gathering pure life energy of nature is the spiritual art referred to as *Bi Gu,* which is fasting to refill higher energy in order to refine one's life and uplift one's spirit. It is not a negative practice of avoiding mortal food, but a way of deriving Immortal Essence from nature at certain points in the cyclic movement of different stars when they are in harmonized positions.

To assist in this, the use of herbal supplements for refining and harmonizing the body, mind and spirit was developed. It is referred to as *Fu Er* or "Reinforcing Energy Through Eating and Drinking By Using Herbs."

6) Then, at an easily attainable level, there is the holistic life art of guiding one's physical energy through a combination of will power and physical exercises in order to gain mastery of the body, breath, internal organs, mind, and life and death. The fundamental techniques include the Yellow Emperor's Energy Guidance, *T'ai Chi Ch'uan*, the Eight Treasures, and related methods of meditation. This science is referred to as *Dao-In* or "Inducing and Guiding Energy Flows Within the Individual Body."

7) The life art of gathering pure, high natural energy in order to reform and refine one's being with food and herbs, referred to as *Fu Chi* or "The Input of Vital Natural Energy" is a highly helpful approach.

8) For the purpose of attaining a higher spiritual life, there is the effective art of transforming spiritual essence through keeping one's thought in accord with the Divine Source. This is referred to as *Chwun Shi* or "Deeply Linking With Divine Thought for Inner Transformation."

9) The correct way of internal alchemy is the immortal art of the mystical conception of a unified spiritual life of wholeness through specific breathing and mental techniques. This method is referred to as *Tai Syi* or "Womb Breathing to Revitalize the Body and Immortalize the Inner Being."

10) There were also very powerful single cultivations such as the spiritual art of embracing transcendental universal oneness in order to nourish one's 'mystical pearl' and accomplish the mystical conception, referred to as *Sau Yi* or "Emerging Into Universal Oneness Through Spiritual Practice."

11) Single external practice is not more effective than uniting both the inner and the outer being. The spiritual art of inner transformation through mystical visualization. "Maintaining the Thought of the Universal Realm" can also produce practical, positive help for one's life.

12) One needs to be careful about the contact one has in life. The spiritual art of purifying one's energy through ascetic practice has the purpose of cleansing one's worldly contamination and altering one's destiny. It is referred to as *Dzai Jing* or "Spiritual Discipline and Prohibition." Doing this periodically is beneficial.

13) To further enhance one's spiritual capability, there is the spiritual art of drawing mystical pictures as a display of power and of writing talismans and reciting powerful sounds and spiritual invocations in order to evoke a response from the subtle realm of the multi-leveled universe. These methods are used to perform exorcism, redeem souls, and subtly control rain, wind, mist and snow.

14) For spiritual education, the spiritual practice of intuitional development through studying the classical scriptures and through direct training from a master's dialogue and contact enables one to dissolve the self and connect with the great whole. It also helps one to develop insight into all spiritual functions of the multi-universe and to harmonize with them.

15) The delicate art of sublimating and refining personal energy for the purpose of revitalization and rejuvenation. To accomplish the integration of both sides of different souls of

an individual, two schools developed. One way is working to achieve immortality through internal efforts; this is the science referred to as '*Nei Dan*,' or the Inner Immortal Medicine. The holistic science of external alchemy for the refinement of golden immortal elixir through the use of rare and undecaying materials. This science is referred to as *Wai Dan* or "External Immortal Medicine," which has brought forth the development of modern chemistry and further advances in alchemy. The other way is to obtain the golden immortal elixir through single or dual cultivation. This science is also referred to as *Nei Dan* or the "Inner Immortal Medicine," which can fortify a person's soul if correctly guided. Usually, people are taught only the holistic science of sexual education for the purpose of enhancing one's health and enjoyment and for balancing one's emotions, referred to as *Fang Jung* or the "Healthy Way of the Inner Room." This is at a different level than what I have described as Internal Medicine. What is popularly known as tantra originated from this practice; it is not a secret, but an education.

16) The system of foreknowledge of an individual's life development uses the five elementary phases and the Big Dipper. Its value is to know one's life potential in order to avoid wasted struggles.

The ancient sages also observed that outward physical manifestations of a person's face, bone structure, palms and voice revealed corresponding inner attitudes and that one's destiny could be seen in those corresponding energy patterns. The natural and subtle influences on an individual's life could be predicted by employing the system of the five subtle phases of energy which occur in regular patterns in time and space.

17) The system of knowledge about the influence of subtle universal energy rays on specific geographic locations, referred to as *Feng Shui* or geomancy, originated when ancient developed ones needed to locate a safe spot for building houses, towns, etc. Different physical locations

on earth have different energy rays and are thus beneficial for different kinds of use or structures. The ability to discern these different rays and their various potencies and to understand how they can support various purposes was greatly valued. Less developed practitioners may not truly know these things by simply observing the operation of the five subtle phases of energy in nature. It is easy to fall prey to superstition. One needs to learn correctly.

18) The pursuit of foreknowledge for specific purposes by arranging and observing the subtle alternations of *yin* and *yang*, was revealed in a system called the *I Ching* or *Book of Changes*. They discovered that by throwing coins, seeds or yarrow sticks in a prescribed manner, one could arrive at a specific arrangement of *yin* and *yang* which would comment on a question asked. In this way, one could determine the consequences of particular events expressed in a symbolic picture. By observing the balance of *yin* and *yang* changes, good decisions could be made regarding military action or the events of daily life. The purpose of practicing the *I Ching* is to learn the balance of movement without following one's impulses toward an extreme and without becoming intellectually assertive. This is a good system for training people to make decisions that are harmonious with the apparent and latent aspects of any situation and to consider the short and long term effects of their actions. Practically speaking, no one should be rigid about the guidance they receive from the *I Ching*, but should value instead the philosophy of balance in individual life as well as great events.

In order to avoid making mistakes and misjudging people one can learn the system of natural energy management and apply it to individual affairs or to national or global matters. This is referred to as *Lyou Yen* and *Chi Men*, the Six Primal *Yang* Water Energies System" and the "Mystical Gates System." These can be positive ways to employ a very subtle arrangement of energy in order to know or change a situation of weakness or dominance in any action or non-action. This enables people to protect themselves and their lands from invaders and avoid becoming ruthless attackers.

"Kind prince, for beginners the common foundation of all effective practices is to study the *I Ching*. This could be a great means of probing both the substantial and insubstantial spheres of life. It is an excellent training process for locating the balance point between a potential conflict between any two sides. It also develops one's ability to handle practical affairs and fosters the evolution of one's mind and spirit. I think the positive value of the *I Ching* is still educational, especially for the complicated life activities of future generations, however, anything concerning a normal, healthy life is the subject of these holistic sciences. They are all instruments for attaining the Universal Way, and all instruments of the Universal Way exist to serve the wholeness of one universal life."

FIFTY-SIX

The master said, "Kind prince, the Way is complete. It is like a big tree with roots, trunk, branches, twigs, leaves, flowers and fruit. Partial practice is not the Universal Integral Way. When one takes any single portion as the whole tree, one creates a distorted worldly religion or a fragmented worldly science. Take the human body for example; it has five senses, two groups of internal organs, four limbs with fingers and toes, etc., all comprising the whole. If one takes a finger or a limb or one of the organs as an object of study, it will create a perspective of dissected details, not the total view. The form and function of a human being come from the integration of all the parts. This is true not only in man but also in the vast multi-universe.

"Kind prince, a big tree with its roots, its trunk, its branches, twigs, flowers and fruit, begins from a tiny seed, just as the multi-universe originates from the invisible particles of energy. All forms come from the formless. The manifest is the subtle performance of the unmanifest. The unmanifest and the manifest become the root of each other as *yin* and *yang* polarities of the integral *T'ai Chi*."

"Venerable Teacher," said the prince, "is it correct to say that everything is the Way?"

"Kind prince, everything that serves the true nature of life is the Way. Everything that does not serve the true nature of life is not the Way. In order to not mislead you I must reveal precisely that everything is the Way and everything is not the Way. To protect and hide oneself under a beautiful concept or to follow a religion and do nothing to serve the world is unvirtuous. It is a sin to enjoy oneself in a monastery all day long, thinking one is practicing holiness. To a person of the Way, everything is the Way. To a person who has disintegrated himself from the Way, everything is not the Way."

FIFTY-SEVEN

The master continued, "There are numberless energy rays or beams with different properties in the universe, including the rays of all the stars, life beings and non-physical life beings in nature. All rays and spirits come from the subtle nature of the universe, and single energy rays or groups of rays relate with and influence everything in their environment. Although these rays never take concrete form, they always exist in the subtle sphere. Without intentional design, the interwoven energy net influences the lives of individual human beings, whole societies and entire races.

"The high energy of the Subtle Origin of the universe is unique and pure. It is absolutely positive, creative and constructive, existing above the twisted realm of duality. The rays of stars and the potency of spirits diversify themselves from the energy ray of the Subtle Origin, and interweave themselves as an intricate, subtle net in all kinds of combinations and interplay. The unintentional influence of the energy rays of the lower spheres of the universe is both positive and negative, constructive and destructive.

"A human soul is composed of various unrefined energy

rays of the universe. Before an individual fully evolves to become a universal being, he may make trouble for himself and others through his unawareness. The full evolution of a human being in the relative sphere is attained through being correctly aware of how to enhance one's positive energy and eliminate subtle negative elements. Through this effort, all human beings can work for their own betterment and the development of a new life.

"A vicious individual is a being who has not yet fully evolved. While completely under the influence of the intricate energy rays and elements within and without, he may bring about disaster for himself and for his surroundings. A virtuous individual who responds to the high, pure, harmonious subtle energy rays and integrates them with the positive elements of his own inner being may strengthen his life, enhance his health and power, and lengthen his years. This is achieved through his own self-cultivation. Then, through his subtle, positive influence, he may help those who are connected with him.

"When one reconnects oneself with the ray of the Subtle Origin of the universe, one can eliminate all negative influences of the conflicting, dualistic lower spheres. The negative influence of the gross spheres of nature is an intricate combination of the energies of stars, massive objects, natural spirits and many other minor influences. Under the extensive influence of this natural force, the undeveloped human mind may be impressed with a domineering image which is like an invisible, tyrannical ruler. This image enhances the aggressive and destructive tendencies of the undeveloped human mind and encourages it to imagine the combined forces of nature as demonic. Both of these misconceptions become strong obstacles to achieving the correct awareness necessary to enlighten a human being. Kind prince, ignore the variation of energy rays and the potency of all kinds of natural spirits. When the Universal Integral Way is applied to one's life, they all merge into harmonious Oneness."

FIFTY-EIGHT

"**K**ind prince, when an individual being or thing loses its balance, either within itself or in relationship to its external environment, its energy becomes incomplete or exhausted and eventually leads to the individual's expiration. Only divine beings have perfect equilibrium and absolute wholeness. This is why they can endure eternally. Thus, the purpose of self-cultivation is to restore the natural integration of body, mind and spirit and to rise above being controlled by biological impulses. This is achieved by balancing *yin* and *yang*, both internally and externally, for in order to evolve to the Universal Realm, one must accomplish the indestructible integration of *yin* and *yang*."

The prince then said, "Venerable Teacher, I now understand that following an extreme theology or imbalanced ideology will lead only to partial development of one's being. Religious sects which emphasize the development of only one aspect of one's being through the rigid practice of extreme austerity, unnatural disciplines or conforming to external dogma lead one nowhere, because these practices contradict the Universal Integral Way of life. Very often what happens when someone tries to cultivate himself in this dichotomous manner is that either the mind becomes the traitor of the body or the body becomes the traitor of the mind. When people cultivate the mind and spirit and disregard the body, the body invariably manifests disharmony by becoming weak or sick. If the body desires sex, one may ignorantly indulge in dissipating sexual activity. If it needs food, one may make ignorant choices of food. One's behavior in these situations undermines one's ideal and factual spiritual achievement.

"If the cultivation of the mind is neglected, it can become like a poisonous snake. One may hope to contain it well, like a snake in a glass cage, but it restlessly looks for a chance to escape every moment. As a result, there is no peace within most people, and this is why when a spiritual peak has been reached, no matter how many times, very few people can maintain it.

"Therefore, if a spiritual path emphasizes the partial development of one aspect of one's being while neglecting the others, its fundamental guidelines are incorrect. These spiritual paths are like helping a drunk walk home; when one side is straightened up, the person falls over to the other side, continually stumbling back and forth. One's entire being must follow one right channel in order to eliminate all contradictions within and without. With the complete cultivation and integration of body, mind and spirit, the external world will reflect one's inner rectification and unity. One will then spontaneously manifest harmony without the need to make any demands on the external world."

"Kind prince, no spiritual peak can be maintained for long. When one experiences spiritual peaks, it is like waking up in the morning, going back to sleep at night, and then waking up again another morning. To a universal being, there is no awakening and no sleeping, no enlightenment and no darkness. A person experiences the events of life, and the experiences of life in turn reveal something about the person. When the person tries to explain the events of his life, this brings about another experience. Thus, although one may be able to describe the events of life, the direct truth of life is different from what is describable. The integral truth of the universe can hardly be put into words."

FIFTY-NINE

"Kind prince, the integral cultivation of immortal achievement must be built on a firm foundation of virtue. The opportunity to learn and practice such cultivation is Heaven's reward to those who are truly virtuous. All human beings are the descendants of the original spiritual inhabitants of this world many, many eons ago, but people have deviated from the accurate awareness of the divine nature of life and have lost the qualities of angelic beings.

Only those who have restored the angelic qualities of their being and who have already actualized the Universal Way may be instructed in the method used by the angels to enhance and integrate their energy in order to become immortal divine beings.

"An individual cannot search for the kind of teacher who is able to instruct him in immortal cultivation, for such teachers reside in the subtle, divine realm or in seclusion where they have an ordinary appearance and lead an ordinary life. It is the teacher who seeks out the student. The experiences an individual manifests are determined by the person's inherent qualities. Therefore, if an individual is interested in receiving instruction from the divine realm regarding his spiritual evolution, he should express his virtuous qualities by extending service to the world. The immortals will then come to the one who is ready.

"Kind prince, it is important to understand that greed for enlightenment and for the secret of immortality is just as great an obstacle for those who aspire to follow the Universal Way as is greed for material wealth. Enlightenment will never come to one who covets it. Instead of desiring to attain high wisdom and know the secret of divine immortality and the mysteries of the universe, one should merely practice indiscriminative virtue. The divine immortals are watching you and guiding you at all times. When your energy is delicate enough and your virtue is powerful enough, the immortals will respond to you. One's high awareness is the true eye of one's being. When you succeed in connecting your energy with the divine realm, the immortals will dwell within you. It is not a matter of anxiously trying to obtain the utmost secrets of life. The transmission of subtle truth is the immortal's reward to the virtuous. All one needs to do is follow the Universal Way of life. Then one will naturally connect oneself with the ultimate truth of the universe. This is the way to become a responsible, fully developed, universal being and an angelic immortal of all times. This is the way all divine ones evolved to the divine realm, and it is the way all universal beings of the future will follow."

SIXTY

"Venerable Teacher, I clearly understand now that the way to become a universal being is to eliminate all concepts of duality from the mind. A universal being can lift himself above the dusty net of worldly contamination at any time. *Yin* and *yang* are the basic principles governing the operation of the universe; there is no specific, dominant power or way. Rigid dogma, therefore, should be avoided both in the life of the individual and by rulers of the masses. Rather than engaging in worldly conflicts concerning fragments of the whole, disciples should remain impartial. This can be achieved, not by taking a neutral or indifferent stance, but by transcending the realm of duality and embracing the natural originalness.

"Dear teacher, you have taught us that the primordial ancestors of the human race were one with the Way and that all of their activities were in harmony with the highest subtle law, but now the worldly way and the spiritual way are no longer one; what is considered normal today was not the normalcy of the universal beings who lived in very ancient times. In what way, therefore, should your disciples cultivate themselves in order to become universal beings?"

"Kind prince," replied the master, "as one grows in self-awareness, one's being evolves from the gross to the subtle, from heavy to light. The continual refinement of personal subtle energy is the precious cultivation of immortal beings. These mystical gems of the technique of immortal achievement will be shown to the one who has completely dissolved the umbilical cord that binds him to the realm of physical energy. All students of life should devote themselves to living a virtuous, integrated life and to accomplishing the transformation of their narrow, superficial personalities. Until this transformation occurs, the mystical door will not open. If it should open prematurely, it would only stir up the person's ambition, tempt him to violate the stability of a normal life and possibly cause him to give up what is important today in exchange for what is important tomorrow. The truth of immortality is the truth of everyday life. Thus, if shallow worldly interest does not die, true evolution of the universal being cannot take place. The keys to the mystical door of divine immortality are given only to those who have transcended all worldly ambition and realized their virtuous fulfillment. These keys have been clearly revealed, but one must go through the different stages of development to understand what the ancient developed ones wrote and taught. An achieved person is one who holds the secret not only of his own life but all of nature. Such a person may roam eternally with and join the unruling rulers and uncreating creators of the multi-universe."

SIXTY-ONE

"Venerable Teacher, if we are worthy enough, would you instruct us how to practice our self-cultivation?"

"Kind prince, long before the beginning of written language, the mystical knowledge of the beginning and development of the universe was directly known by the very ancient developed ones whose minds were one with the Universal Mind. It was revealed that the developing universe is the expression of its subtle nature which is the same reality as the subtle truth of being and non-being and the subtle law of all existence and non-existence. This development and its law is not the same thing as the duality of law-makers and followers in the human world. The development of the universe is its own law, its own reason and its own way as the totality of one life. Therefore, to the narrative mind it is unnameable and beyond description. In other words, by looking at the outer physical universe and its movements one can discover the physical universe and its mechanisms. With developed vision, spiritually developed ones can see the law, the truth, reason and way of the self-born, self-operating, self-generating and regenerating essence of the multi-natural world and use simple language to call it 'the Way.' The Way does not exist sometime or somewhere else, but is everywhere and at all times now. From the perception of the developed vision of the whole, the first divisions of manifestation from the Subtle One were called *yin* and *yang*, *yin* being the physical manifestation that is symbolized by a broken line (▬ ▬), while manifestation of subtle energy, or *yang*, is symbolized by an unbroken line (▬▬). The integration of these two was called *T'ai Chi* ☯ .

"A human being is a model of the integration of *yin* and *yang*, with physical energy manifesting as the body and subtle energy manifesting as the mind and spirit. Further, the ancients referred to these three aspects of the universe as Heaven (symbolized by three solid lines ☰) which is *yang*, Earth (symbolized by three broken lines ☷) which is *yin*, and Man (symbolized by *T'ai Chi* ☯) which is the integration of the *yin* and *yang*.

"The ancient sages also expressed the development of the universe numerically. The number one represented the Subtle Origin, while two represented the duality of *yin* and *yang*, and three the trinity of *yin*, *yang* and their integration as *T'ai Chi*, which brings forth life. These are considered the three main categories of the Universe.

"The number four represents the four basic forces of the universe which are variations of *yin* and *yang*: the strong force which was referred to as 'old *yang*' ☰); the weak force which was called 'old *yin*' (☷); the heavy force which was called 'young *yang*' (☳); and the light force which was called 'young *yin*' ☴). For a force to be strong does not necessarily mean that it is heavy, nor is a weak force necessarily light. It is possible for a force to be both light and strong or weak and heavy. These four forces may be considered as parallels to what modern physics terms 'strong nuclear force'(☰), 'gravity' (☳), 'weak nuclear force' (☷), and 'electromagnetism' (☴). The harmonization of these four forces creates a fifth, united force, a *T'ai Chi*, which is the harmonizing force of the universe, a common field. The ancient sages called all five forces the Five Great Performers of the Universe (*Wu Hsing*), and symbolized them with five physical manifestations. Water symbolized the strong force characterized by aggregation, contraction, collection and condensation. Fire symbolized the weak force characterized by expansion, disaggregation, dispersion and dissipation. Wood symbolized the light force characterized by explosion and dynamism. Metal symbolized the heavy force characterized by gravity. The inherent nature of these four different forces battle and conquer each other, while earth symbolizes the united, harmonized and neutral force among them.

"The Five Great Performers are a very useful system in the practice of internal alchemy. Fire symbolizes mental energy or spirit; water symbolizes sexual energy or general vitality; wood symbolizes male energy; metal symbolizes female energy. Earth harmonizes all incompatible pairs of energy and works as an intermediary between them; it enables the integration of all forces as a *T'ai Chi*. The Mystical Pass appears to one who has practiced internal alchemy as the Five Performers disintegrate at the culmination of life in the physical realm. The Mystical Pass is the key enabling a breakthrough into the immortal realm. This is the great transformation of a human life from the gross realm of the cycle of life and death to the exquisite realm of absolute freedom and eternal life.

"One can achieve this transformation not through attempting to create a way, but through discovering the way. Human beings cannot create anything on the subtle level outside of their beings. They can give birth to spiritual entities which would become the composite elements of their new life in the spiritual realm. However, through breaking away from the old and connecting with the new, one may spiritually outlive one's physical life. With developed vision one discovers the mystical keys which unlock the secrets of spiritual life in the multi-universe and the universe of natural and orderly progression. To understand the orderly world, the first key is *T'ai Chi*, the ultimate truth of existence; the second is the Great Two, displayed as a parade of *yin* and *yang*; the third is the Three Main Categories expressed by Heaven, Earth and Man; the fourth is the Four Forces, the strong force, the weak force, the light force and the heavy; the fifth is the Five Great Performers of the Universe symbolized by water, fire, wood, metal and earth; the sixth is the Six *Chi* or Six Breaths which manifest as *Tai Yang* ☰), *Shao Yang* (☳), *Yang Ming* (☲), *Tai Yin* (☷), *Shao Yin* (☵), and *Chiu Yin* (☴) which express themselves in the transformation of the human organs and as climatic influences of wind, cold, heat, moisture, dryness and inflammation.

"The seventh key is the process of change and recycling. The eighth is the Eight Great Manifestations:

☰	☷	☵	☲
Heaven	Earth	Water	Fire
☳	☱	☴	☶
Thunder	Lake	Wind	Mountain

with vast categories of each as the Great Transformations of the Universe. The Eight Great Transformations generate the sixty-four hexagrams with three hundred and eighty-four lines which display all possible combinations of *yin* and *yang*. These important systems reveal the truth of Nature and the ways of manifesting all situations and self-transformations of life. There are also many other profound diagrams which help unlock the mystical gate of the subtle evolution of the universe, of human history and of individual lives. Some diagrams will be shown to help illustrate these systems.

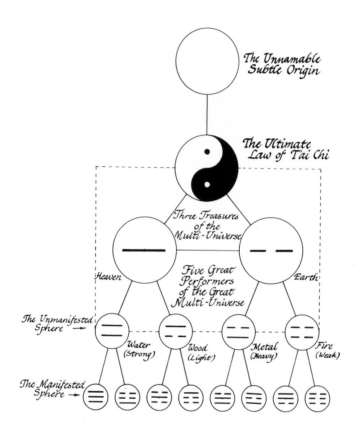

The Unnamable
Subtle Origin

The Ultimate
Law of Tai Chi

Three Treasures
of the
Multi-Universe

Five Great
Performers
of the Great
Multi-Universe

Heaven   Earth

The Unmanifested
Sphere →

Water   Wood   Metal   Fire
(Strong)   (Light)   (Heavy)   (Weak)

The Manifested
Sphere →

From the Subtle Origin
to Infinity

Yin & Yang developing into
Four Forces & then Eight Great Manifestations

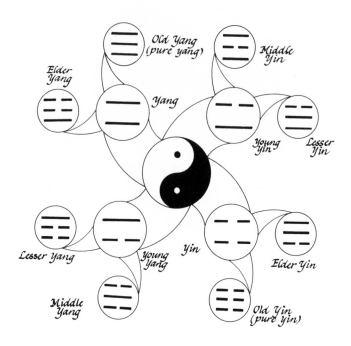

The center part of the Sixty-four Dimensions

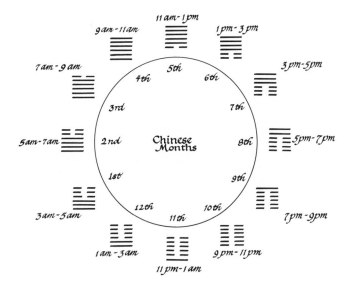

Energy Cycle based on Time Sequence

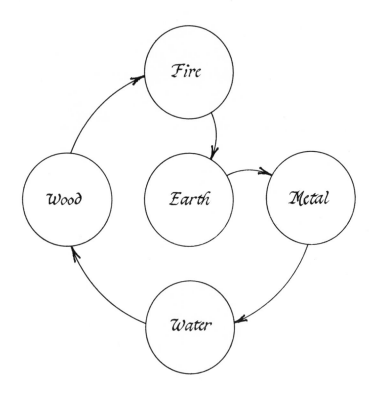

Normal & Regular Cycle of Energy Flow

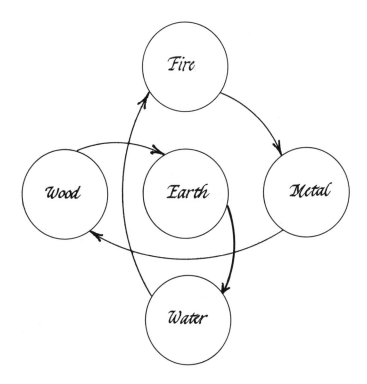

Abnormal Cycle of Energy Flow

SIXTY-TWO

"Venerable Teacher," asked the wise prince, "may I know something more about the Three Main Categories of the multi-universe?"

"Kind prince, the development of a human being's inner vision corresponds to his spiritual evolution throughout many lifetimes. There are a few individuals who have achieved a complete vision of the multi-universe, especially the whole truth of the Three Main Categories which are the most essential and profound truth of the expansion and exhibition of the vast multi-universe."

"Venerable Teacher, I have discovered that as my inner vision expands its range, the universe seems to expand also. This process is similar to the way in which the traditional healing points were discovered; the points were always there, but with experience generation after generation discovered more and more points and groups of points to use in healing practices."

"Kind prince, your intention to know more about the Three Main Categories is commendable. Truly, the inner vision of the multi-universe was intuitively developed through many generations of people of whole vision, similar, as you say, to the way in which the energy points of the body were discovered. It is important to understand, however, that these truths were merely discoveries and not inventions of the human mind. The human mind is incapable of inventing or creating anything as its own contribution to the divine order of the universe.

"Kind prince, the unfolding of one's inner vision is a natural process which corresponds with the inner growth of the individual. It happens spontaneously. If one tries to formalize discoveries of spiritual truth into rigid doctrines to be taught to others as a means of establishing a train of followers, then one will invariably mislead people and impair their inner growth. If people take these truths for granted, their significance is diminished and they become mere emotional tranquilizers for the undeveloped majority of mankind.

"These discoveries were passed down as a standard of individual development by people whose inner vision had become connected to the entire truth of the universe. I am willing to give you the outline, but I will leave the details of this knowledge to be completed by those who truly cultivate and develop themselves."

"Venerable Teacher, may I know why Heaven is considered one of the Three Treasures?"

"Kind prince, the total reality of the universe is energy; it is called 'prime energy' or 'prime chi.' Two divisions of this energy occur: the heavy, physical energy of the earth and the light, spiritual energy of heaven. The three divisions of this energy are the physical, the spiritual and a combination of the two.

"Human life represents one whole category of the natural energy flow. The ancient developed ones used the three divisions of energy to distinguish the energy in an individual human being: spiritual energy being centered in the head, physical energy in the belly, and harmonized energy in the heart and mind.

"Spiritual energy is not equally pure at all levels, and each of the Three Main categories has its own purity: *Yu Ching, Shan Ching* and *T'ai Ching.* As we have already seen, these unified energies can be applied to both the macrocosm and the microcosm. To the ancient achieved ones, the purity of the three different levels was the goal of personal achievement. One who achieved himself spiritually attained the range of *Yu Ching*; one who achieved himself by attaining the wisdom that is connected with universal mindedness or universal heartedness attained the range of *Shan Ching*; and one who achieved himself by refining his sexual energy attained the range of *T'ai Ching.* The one who achieved himself with all three, expressed in an integral and virtuous life, attained the Universal Integral Way.

"Kind prince, an individual's very being is composed of all the various energies of the universe which are expressed in the different physical characteristics and inherent subtle attributes of human life. These differences are clues to the subtle origin of the energies of the individual and to the origin of nature.

"An individual human being is a small model of the multi-universe, with a hidden and profound nature that is connected to the heavenly realms. Nevertheless, the development of most human beings follows a narrow track which makes them partial and incomplete and thus causes them to lose their appreciation for the great variety that composes the unity of nature."

"Venerable Teacher, I deeply appreciate the completeness of the spiritual achievement of the ancient developed ones, and I admire their complete inner vision."

SIXTY-THREE

"Kind prince," said the master, "Heaven is another name for the three Realms of Purity. It is, therefore, a triad within the triad of the universe. Earth and Man are also parts of the greater triad as well as triads in and of themselves.

"In the three Main Categories of the multi-universe, the Realm of Great Purity, 'T'ai Ching,' is where the productive earth and myriad things reside. It is the lower or outer sphere of nature. The Realm of High Purity, 'Shan Ching,' is where the subtle mind resides; it is the middle sphere. The Realm of Ultimate Purity, 'Yu Ching,' is the residence of the immortal, divine beings and the most exquisite energy of the universe. All three of these spheres are generated from and rooted in one chi, the Divine Subtle Origin.

"In the achievement of a spiritually developed being, the mode of being in the Realm of T'ai Ching is three dimensional and has three components: 'Hsiang,' pure appearance; 'Chi,' natural, healthy, vital energy; and 'Li,' pure law and reason.

"When one reaches the Realm of Shan Ching, the layer of gross, material form is ineffective and the mode of being further harmonizes Hsiang, Chi, and Li. The beings of this realm are still individually distinguishable, however.

"When one reaches *Yu Ching*, the Realm of *Li* or pure law, there is no confinement by the distinction of *Chi* and no rigidity of material force or form. The beings of this realm have complete freedom, for they are one with pure law. The life of a being in this realm is absolutely straight and direct. If there is any slight crookedness of being, or even a slight deviation or separation from *Li*, the being is immediately downgraded to the realm of duality and subjected to the control of the two laws of *Chi* and *Li*; he is the servant of these two masters. The further the being is downgraded, the more physical law is imposed. The further the downfall of a person, the more forces he is subjected to and bound by in the form of laws. This includes the multiple bondage of material, flesh-centered life.

"At a certain stage the societies of certain tribes of the human race were unlawful. Civilization brings law, but in an evolved society of developed individuals moral law is a matter of common commitment among all people. Once one lifts oneself above all grossness and contamination within one's own being, pure law may manifest itself again. This is the way to become one with pure law.

"Kind prince, within the Three Realms of Great Nature there are numerous small universes. Each of these is called a 'cave universe,' and this physical universe is one of those. To the undeveloped, the universe is an isolated world. Insulated by darkness, the beings who live in one cave universe are unaware of the existence of other cave universes. A highly evolved being, however, can break through the bondage of many layers of darkness.

"Kind prince, non-impulsiveness is the highest expression of a universal being. All high virtues are accomplished within this pure law, but do you think there are many who are able to follow it? No, kind prince. Worldly people are restless and impulsive, they suffer from their lack of self-control and thus evoke many laws. Highly evolved people have their own conscience as pure law.

"Most people are born with heavy, gross energy and live

their lives in bondage to the laws of the material plane. The more restless a person becomes, the stronger the bondage will be. In order to cooperate with pure law, quiescence must be established and maintained. By not touching the gross world and by avoiding any strife they are saved from bondage.

"Kind prince, the truth of the universe is uncovered when one simplifies all aspects of one's life. Simplification is the highest discipline of this sacred tradition. Refinement of one's personality and the channeling of one's refined sexual energy upwards to the higher centers of one's being is the method of true evolution. There are very few people who are able to evolve highly. By breaking through all hindrances step by step, they gradually come to the Realm of High Purity. At first they go up and down with uncertainty and instability until they completely uplift themselves. Then, layer by layer, they evolve to higher and higher planes.

"The integration of *yin* and *yang* and the elimination of all mental duality are the real vehicles of immortal life. The Universal Integral Way is simple to understand and easy to follow, yet people wander away from their universal nature and become lost in ideological and theological mists of their own creation. Once one knows to stop this wandering and return to simplicity, the Universal Way of the angels reappears once again. When the lost wanderer returns to his divine origin, integral universal awareness will bring him great reward."

SIXTY-FOUR

"Venerable Teacher, would you instruct us in how we may cultivate ourselves so that we may have contact with the subtle truth of the multi-universe?"

"Kind prince, people whose intellects are overly developed or who are skeptical about the subtle truth can effectively restore the wholeness of their minds through integrating the internal and external elements of their being. The way to achieve this integration is to learn how to evoke a specific response from the subtle energy of the universe. A good and available tool for the public is the 'Observation of the Changing Signs.' By using specific methods, with an uncalculating mental attitude, an individual can discover the subtle alternations of *yin* and *yang* which operate within and influence all events of life. In order to evoke an accurate manifestation from the subtle energy when inquiring into the changing signs, one must regulate one's mind, for a regulated mind is the power which manifests an accurate response in physical terms. A clear mind is the eye of one's being, while a confused mind blinds one's true eye.

"Every single event that occurs in the universe is a *T'ai Chi* containing both *yin* and *yang*, and all individual events combine into one great event which is also a *T'ai Chi*. The alternation of *yin* and *yang* is the inevitable truth of the universe. This natural phenomenon is clearly observable in the alternation of day and night; however, in many areas of life the alternation is not so easy to observe. The Observation of the Changing Signs is a method which enables one to determine how to be in harmony with the subtle laws of the universe in all activities of life. The changing signs indicate the alternation of *yin* and *yang* in specific circumstances; by learning to recognize, classify, understand and utilize them with the rational mind and also with one's intuition, one may learn to deal with all circumstances that occur in life. This is only the superficial use of the Observation of the Changing Signs, however. The highest use of these principles lies in using them to harmonize all the elements of one's being and return to a state of universal oneness.

"Kind prince, the universal beings of the primordial communities of Earth knew no strife, either among themselves or with the rest of the world. In all of their activities they did nothing to violate the subtle alternation of *yin* and *yang*, but lived in harmony with their natural and social environment. There was no need, therefore, to develop methods of obtaining foreknowledge. As time passed, however, people began to deviate from their integral, universal nature and it became necessary for them to practice the Observation of the Changing Signs, especially when making decisions about important matters such as military action, hunting expeditions, marriage and so forth. With the information they received from the Observation of the Changing Signs they were able to make decisions that were in harmony with natural law and therefore avoid unnecessary trouble and sacrifice.

"Kind prince, in the multi-universe, the high truth known as the Way is the only thing that gives great constancy. Everything else is governed by the great law of transformation. The invariable Way is the constant nature of the universe, yet within it is contained the variability of the myriad things. Through observing the changes in the myriad things, one may come to recognize the constancy of the subtle law, for the myriad things are merely variations of the one, original chi. The deep and subtle essence behind all change is constancy. Kind prince, with spiritual cultivation, the awareness of the subtle alternations of *yin* and *yang* becomes deeper and deeper. Through searching for the changeless element that exists behind the myriad fluctuations, one may discover the source of all variation, the key to the great transformation. In this way, one uses variation to find the immutable; once the immutable is discovered, one may embrace it.

"By uniting one's being with the constant creative nature of the universe, one may achieve mastery of the great law of transformation in all spheres of life. This is how the Universal Way is discovered and the state of duality transcended. The restless and inquisitive mind will be dissolved and find true peace through complete union with the Way.

"Kind prince, if the mind of a person who uses the predictive method of Observation of the Changing Signs is only partially developed, the benefit he derives will be very limited. To be motivated by the desire to know only whether one will gain or lose something in the material sphere of life is to limit oneself by the bounds of one's own self interest.

If these methods become the tool of egotism and selfishness, they could even become dangerous. Yet, if one's mind is fully developed and one uses subtle knowledge for the purpose of achieving Oneness, one will be nurtured through the understanding of the complete truth.

"Kind prince, when the long age of confusion begins, people will undertake important endeavors, guided only by their own impulses. They will no longer refer to predictive methods for determining whether their actions will be in harmony with the subtle law; this art will be lost to the masses. Yet, even in the confused times of the future, the ancient predictive arts will be a testable way for people to return to the integrity of their own being. By developing the ability to know the future by knowing the subtle pictures formalized in one's own mind, people may rediscover how to live in harmony and how to control the negative tendencies of the mind.

"The great self-examining systems of this ancient tradition can guide all the young lives to study and to reach self-development; this is what it takes to uplift oneself. If the entire system is studied and its principles understood, one will gradually achieve mastery of the whole truth, knowing even the non-existent parts of an event. Every event is the necessary result of external decisive factors and the subtle picture in the subjective mind. It is not hard to recognize the influence that comes about through the harmony or disharmony between the subjective mind and objective fact.

"In general situations, people can exercise their free will to engage in a not-wholly-developed matter. But, if free will is recognized, the responsibility of success and failure belongs to the one who exercises his free will. For the most part, it should be the person himself who forms his mind and his future through cultivating the mind, refining the personality and adjusting attitudes toward challenging external situations.

"Kind prince, the self-examining systems are only one aspect of the 'discipline of flexibility' of this ancient spiritual art. It is important to remember that a good predictive method is a tool for reaching out beyond the limited realm of the mind. Above this level lies the boundless and profound ocean of spirit which cannot be touched by the mind. The attainment of the highest mental and spiritual levels requires very deep involvement and commitment. Only through total dedication to one's spiritual evolution can one lift oneself to the integral oneness of the Subtle Origin, the Way."

SIXTY-FIVE

"Venerable teacher, in all of our discussions it would seem that the human mind is capable of being as familiar with the entire universe as it is with the fingers and palm of one's own hand. It seems as if there is nothing that can escape the observation of the human eye and the penetration of the developed human mind."

"Kind prince," replied the master, "the truth is that the only thing that can be perceived with the senses is the thin shell of reality. The physical universe in which people live is merely the small but important reproductive vision of the divine Mysterious Mother. All of the galaxies, nebulae, stars, planets and other heavenly bodies exist in the outer wall of the Mysterious Mother's womb. The interplay of *yin* and *yang* creates the expansion and contraction of nature and brings forth all things. This interplay of *yin* and *yang*, however, expresses the creative universal nature which is behind the movement.

"The whole being of the great goddess is of an unfathomable depth. The Universal Heart is her heart and the Divine Pure Law is her pure being.

"Most of humanity starts and ends in the first stage of life, centered around the reproductive organs, without looking for any further development. Its life activities are still at the stage of being which produces seeds and eggs whose behavior is determined by blind, biological impulse. Such lives are limited to the link with the mystical reproductive valley of the Mysterious Mother, but have not yet reached the center where high reason is activated.

"Union of *yin* and *yang* brings forth the manifestation of life, while their disintegration results in the manifestation of death. As life evolves from the lowest level of the one-celled organism to the human level where two genders are clearly distinguishable, the incompleteness of *yin* and *yang* energies within an individual becomes more obvious. On the physical level, the very essences of life need to be paired in order to produce a new life. Although a human being appears to be complete and independent, in truth, one's energy is not complete. Individuals need to pair themselves to complete and unite the *yin* and *yang* energies within themselves in order to bring forth a new life. When an individual's subtle *yin* and *yang* energies are refined and indestructibly integrated, he is born into a higher plane of immortal life.

"Kind prince, people become bewildered by the myriad manifestations of the physical sphere of the universe. They dissect the world into small parts and perceive only fragments of the physical environment. They see only the bushes and not the forest. All exploration and adventure in the ordinary sense never go beyond the reproductive sphere of the universe; the divine being of the Mysterious Mother is never reached by most people. Only those who are very highly evolved have the opportunity to break through all obstructions and reach the universal-heartedness and pure reason of the Mysterious Mother."

SIXTY-SIX

"Kind prince, all life is brought forth as a result of the integration of *yin* and *yang*. When a seed and an egg unite within a female, a new life is conceived. This is the first integration of *yin* and *yang* in the human sphere. The second integration of *yin* and *yang* takes place when the physically mature male and female interrelate sexually. This union may bring about the integration of *yin* and *yang*, but it may not bring about the integration of the egg and the seed of each partner. It may appear to ordinary eyes that the birth of a human being is the beginning of a new life, but a human life at this stage of development has not yet been born into the spiritual light which is characterized by complete understanding and high wisdom. Unless an individual is born into the immortal realm, a third integration of *yin* and *yang* cannot happen.

"Life in the physical sphere is a preparation for birth into the subtle realm. Everything born into the physical world must die; however, a developed individual who learns the Immortal Way may be born again into a life of absolute freedom. A subtle transformation takes place within an individual when he succeeds in cultivating himself and attains pure wisdom. Immortal cultivation is a gradual process of practicing pure diet, energy conducting exercises (*Tow ying*), and the cultivation and refinement of one's whole being (*Shu Liang*). With this the heavy, gross energy of one's life begins to diminish. All of these practices are the preparation for breaking through the cycle of birth, procreation and death, and emerging into the immortal divine one.

"As an individual's energy becomes more refined and subtle, he comes under the dominant control of the physical realm less and less. As such a life evolves, it gradually becomes submerged in the mighty ocean of spiritual energy, the Universal Divine Energy, and a new life, governed by wisdom rather than emotion, is thus created. As one's sense of life broadens, the psychological ego is dissolved and the entire body is positively influenced. As one subtly transforms oneself, one leaves the gross realm and approaches immortal divinity. The evolution of the soul depends on the growth of self-awareness. This takes place over the course of many lifetimes through learning the Integral Way of the universe and following the precise and explicit methods of self-cultivation which are the heritage of the accomplished angels. The third integration of *yin* and *yang* is the mystical conception of a new immortal life.

"Kind prince, life which is born of flesh and blood must inevitably die. Life which is born by cultivating the integration of the subtle energies of *yin* and *yang* never dies. Although every human life begins with the integration of *yin* and *yang*, life produces continual self-splitting in a geometric progression, expressed by the *I Ching* as pure whole energy splitting itself into ' ▬▬ ' and ' ▬ ▬ '. There is then further endless progression and finally complete disintegration. The possibility of achieving immortal life lies in restoring the integration of *yin* and *yang* and becoming whole once again. Immortality comes with the practice of virtue that embraces the essence of all life."

SIXTY-SEVEN

"Venerable Teacher, it is my firm and immutable decision to follow the Universal Way as the only guidance in my life and to practice the integration of *yin* and *yang* as my self-cultivation so that my life will be a complete model of *T'ai Chi*.

"The way to integrate my own *yin* and *yang* is to discard all lofty and fanciful thinking and argumentative discussion and to follow the invariable principles of universal truth. If I must practice cultivation by myself, I will steadily move through all the phases of spiritual evolution step by step. The individual practice of self-cultivation is the foundation of all high spiritual achievement, just as you have taught us. Nature supplies me with physical vitality, just as she supplies it to all life at the biological level. I will sublimate my sexual energy so that it becomes wisdom, and then transform my wisdom into immortal spirit.

"If blessing is afforded to me, if Heaven allows me, and if my virtue sufficiently supports me, I shall be instructed in the practice of final individual self-integration. If it is suitable to practice dual cultivation, I may experience the direct integration of *T'ai Chi* through the intersection of doubled *yin* and *yang*. If my virtue does not support me, if my blessing limits me and if I do not bring any virtuous merit to the world through serving others, I still will be a person of natural integration without doing any harm to my life, if that is possible. Sometime I hope to receive the secret of dual cultivation, for without correct guidance it would only be an abuse that would cause my downfall and ruin my opportunity to achieve immortality rather than fulfill its positive purpose."

The master replied, "Kind prince, the practice of dual cultivation has many different purposes and levels. One is to balance one's energy, for when one's energy is balanced, one's health improves, one's emotions are harmonious, and one's personality becomes smooth and even. Although this certainly has a positive value, its benefit is on a general level. Dual cultivation can be a mental and spiritual discipline, which leads to the achievement of desirelessness. If a person exposes himself to that which is desirable, can he find out if he has transcended desire and refined his impulses?

"At the highest level of dual cultivation, however, one faces differences in energy in order to integrate what one already has within and to bring about a transcendent integration of one's own energy. The form of intercourse is not even necessary in order to achieve immortality.

"The opportunity and the secret to achieving immortality is a reward for someone who has achieved truly great virtue. In the long history of this tradition, such things are taught by the divine immortals to the follower who is able to learn the precious secret of achieving total integration. Even though a person may be boundlessly virtuous, he must also harmonize his life being. Although every human being is an integration of *yin* and *yang*, further uniting of *yin* and *yang* is necessary for the conception of a higher life. High beings need to continually combine new spheres of *yin* and *yang* in order to achieve still higher spheres of life. Thus, an individual may need to practice dual cultivation so that he may complete his energy. In the secret method of harmonization of *yin* and *yang*, the great sun is the male energy for all the female students. Male students may also utilize solar energy to assist their weakened male energy. It does not mean one should live like an animal, just that one must have sufficient *yang* energy. The earth and the moon are abundant sources of female energy that male students can utilize to support their balance and achieve long, healthy lives. There are some further details for guiding one's energy cultivation. For example, lakes symbolize young female energy, hills symbolize young male energy, etc. These are the potent knowledge and techniques of historical practitioners of natural harmony. The highest qualification of the practitioner in the union of male and female is something I consider a secret of secondary importance, because not many people are able to utilize it. For those of truly great virtue who do not have the opportunity to learn the secret of dual cultivation, the Universal Divine Energy will provide the remedy to support, supplement and complete their energy."

SIXTY-EIGHT

"Venerable Teacher, may I ask what are the primary principles of angelic dual cultivation?"

"Kind prince, listen well. The primary principles of angelic dual and single cultivation are contained in these lines which were revealed to me by the immortal beings:

One of integral virtue follows the subtle law
and the subtle law alone.
The subtle energy of the universe is elusive and evasive.
It unveils itself in images and forms.
Evasive and elusive,
it discloses itself as indefinable substance.
Shadowy and indistinct,
it further reveals itself
as impalpable subtle essence
which is so subtle, yet so real.

With unfailing sincerity
   one may know and rejoin this subtle reality.
Returning to itself
   is how the eternal subtle essence exercises itself.
Being gentle and yielding
   is how the subtle essence employs itself.
All things come from the Manifest,
   and the Manifest comes from the Unmanifest.
The softest of all things
   can overcome the hardest of all things.
Only the insubstantial can penetrate the spaceless.
Thus I know the benefit of non-action and silence.
There are few under Heaven who can attain it.

"Kind prince, those are the primary principles of angelic dual and single cultivation. Learn them well, meditate on them and apply them carefully with correct understanding throughout the interplay of *yin* and *yang* in your single or dual cultivation."

SIXTY-NINE

"Kind teacher,' said the prince, "to most people, sexuality is one of the main activities of life. I would like to know some of the spiritual sexual guidance that can help those who wish to lift themselves from the lower level of animal impulse to the higher level of energy integration."

"Kind prince," said the master, "an individual's approach to sexuality is an indication of his level of evolution. There is a vast difference between ordinary human sexual activity and the dual cultivation of a practitioner of natural harmony. In ordinary intercourse, the sexual organs take primary importance while the other organs and systems of the body are subordinate. In this way, the servant controls the master, and then one's energy dissipates and becomes disordered.

"Every cell of an individual's being seeks the union of *yin* and *yang*, not merely the sexual organs. The purpose of angelic intercourse is the union and completion of an individual's *yin* and *yang* energy. It is a process of refinement and sublimation of energy. Once the energy is refined, it is directed upward to the higher centers of one's being. In angelic intercourse, spirit unites with spirit, mind with mind, and every cell of one body with every cell of the other body. It is the spirit, not the sexual organs, which directs such intercourse.

"Another difference is that ordinary intercourse seeks a substantial manifestation as its culmination, while angelic intercourse seeks the intangible union of *yin* and *yang*. Angelic intercourse is not completed by a substantial discharge, but rather with the integration of each partner's subtle energy. In this way, angelic intercourse leads to immortality.

"Ordinary intercourse requires making an effort, but in angelic intercourse the love union is achieved spontaneously through the male's non-action. When one remains very calm and relaxed, the gross sexual impulse diminishes and the subtle energy becomes more developed. The great, subtle transformation takes place naturally and in silence. The whole universe is developed in this way. It happens naturally, not through making it happen.

"In preparation for this sacred instruction, every disciple must extend his virtue to the world in order to accomplish the mission of world peace and purification. One should learn the immortal truth of life. If one extends one's virtue selflessly to the world, the immortal truth will unite with one naturally. The general principles of achieving energy integration have been shown, but the details are usually taught directly by a teacher who has truly achieved himself. By following the right channel of life and by radiating a virtuous influence to the world, one may develop one's subtle energy. In this way one can reconnect oneself with the subtle realms, and the immortals will give their guidance even without a teacher.

"The secret immortal practice is to turn external sexual intercourse inwardly to the mind and body. When the union of the essence of the mind and the essence of the body occurs, one is truly achieved in this very simple way."

SEVENTY

"**K**ind prince, dual cultivation is a key which can enable individuals in the physical realm to realize true liberation. In general, the life of a human being is a complex net woven out of the threads of passion and desire. A person thinks that every single thread is necessary, never realizing the slow, inexorable process of enslavement that is being woven about him. Through reflective self-awareness, one can unravel this self-woven net and free himself from the servitude into which his passionate actions and desires have led him. Once freed of the lower traps of *yin* and *yang* duality, one may live naturally, work virtuously without succumbing to egotism, and regain eternal vitality. Through strict regulation of one's activities and creativity, one may become reconnected with the realm of being which enriches one with great potency and in which there are no obstructions. If a person succeeds in this reconnection, he ceases to be a slave and achieves full independence and spiritual autonomy. Kind prince, freedom is not a gift that is given to the individual; it is a task of self-transformation and subjective evolution.

"An individual has the possibility of vanquishing death and rising to the highest realms of being through attracting *yang* energy from the source of universal life. In order to accomplish this, he must dissolve his *yin* energy into the luminous substance from which his subtle essence has descended. In this realm of being he is permanently out of danger of relapsing into the cycle of rebirth. In this realm it is no longer important to have the sense of an individual soul or spirit as the substance of one's life, for one's life is pure nature itself, the constancy of the universe.

"Kind prince, it is essential to understand that an individual must remain one with the constant virtue of life and dissolve the stiffness and rigidity gathered by worldly confrontation. When the internal metamorphosis is complete, he may emerge into a new realm of being in which he is one with Tao. This is the culmination of his evolution into the realm of pure freedom."

SEVENTY-ONE

"Venerable Teacher, all of your disciples are fortunate to have the rare opportunity of receiving this precious instruction directly from you. Many generations from now, during the time of confusion, will people have the opportunity to learn the verbal and non-verbal teachings of this sacred tradition?"

"Kind prince, only after people refine their heavy, gross energy and reach the subtle level can they attain self-mastery. Only after they have attained self-mastery can the principles of self-integration through single or dual cultivation and the unworded teaching be passed on to them. Only then will they be able to derive the benefit of them.

"During the process of purifying the body, mind and spirit, the gradual transformation toward eternal life occurs. If a teacher instructs a person who has not yet achieved purification and self-mastery, the energy of desire will cause trouble and conflict. Therefore, the careless, general dissemination of this teaching of pure being is not encouraged."

The prince said, "Venerable Teacher, I understand that one who has the opportunity to learn self-cultivation and dual cultivation should maintain right practice in order to achieve spiritual freedom and transcend the dualistic trap of life."

"Kind prince, the tempting angelic dual cultivation is not an exclusive practice. For the purpose of energy balance, sometimes it is a remedy to a weakened male if correctly guided, however all practices and disciplines should be parallel practices; one assists the other. Just as a balance between eating, drinking, and fasting enables one to maintain health, celibacy and dual cultivation work together to enable one to attain internal and external harmony. For reasons of different energy formation in each individual, however, celibacy may be more appropriate than dual cultivation for some people, while for others periodic celibacy is very uplifting. When and how to use these methods may be determined through the guidance of a developed teacher. The highest principle to be followed in spiritual practice is that of energy response; the safest and most effective method is not safe and effective if the natural energy does not harmoniously respond. One's achievement must come from connecting oneself with the Universal Divine Energy; teachers and techniques are but transitional."

SEVENTY-TWO

"Venerable Teacher, I am very eager to learn the way to enter the divine realm with great spiritual power, and I am willing to undergo the most stringent purification to become truly worthy of receiving this sacred and precious teaching."

"Kind prince, any merit attained must have come about through extending one's virtue to the world, and any spiritual achievement must have been through self-cultivation and union with the original Oneness. This means not engaging in schemes which would separate one from the Universal Integral Way and not forming impulsive ambitions that would cause the loss of wholeness of the mind. The pure mind is an exquisite energy in human life. It is an important part in one's life being with which to cultivate and achieve divine immortality through the virtuous power of kindness, tolerance and patience. In order to be correct, one's self-cultivation must have as its purpose the integration of one's being with the universal virtuous energy which is the true and durable spiritual energy of the universe. people with a high capability can achieve higher spiritually by doing some ordinary daily work such as healing, but not through imaginary magic for the purpose of satisfying their undeveloped emotions. To compose all virtues into one reality entails developing and extending the virtue one already has; there is no virtue that is not already contained within one's own nature.

"To embrace the universal Oneness, one must not let circumstances of any kind seize one's mind, nor should one let one's mind become so preoccupied that one loses all awareness of present circumstances. On the Universal Way, there is neither mind nor circumstances. There is nothing, and there is no attachment to the nothingness. This is the way to manage one's mind in daily life, whether practicing single or dual cultivation. Only through the elimination of all strife can Universal Oneness be attained."

"Venerable Teacher," asked the prince, "is angelic dual cultivation virtuous?"

"Kind prince, angelic dual cultivation is virtuous if practiced correctly and unvirtuous if practiced incorrectly. It is an opportunity for a man and woman to uplift each other spiritually and enjoy the bliss of wholeness."

"Venerable Teacher," asked the prince again, "is marriage suitable for all spiritual people?"

"Kind prince, marriage is a social structure which came about in later generations of human development. It should be duly respected and recognized as a foundation of human society, but dual cultivation relies on mutual energy response through divine guidance. It is not motivated by sexual impulse or by the need for financial cooperation in life, but only by spiritual purposes."

SEVENTY-THREE

"Venerable Teacher, should a disciple offer his or her energy to the master in dual cultivation?"

"Kind prince, all teachers and their disciples should offer their talent, wealth and life to the world. The teacher is the one who offers himself or herself to the disciples. The disciples are his or her world. Between the teacher and disciples is an interplay of spiritual dedication in which the one who is offering cannot be distinguished from the one who is receiving. It is not even possible to distinguish who is the teacher and who is the student. Achieved minds are simply mirrors reflecting one another. The pure energy of a student may be offered to the angels who dwell within the master. Those whose energy is depleted should offer fresh flowers, young plants, newly opened wine and freshly made food, as well as their service, to symbolize and express their spiritual offering. Those who make offerings to the master without self-restraint are blessed with the actualization of breaking away from their physical individuality to live inside of each other. This joy can only happen among selfless beings with pure spiritual devotion. Any small suspicions or jealousy would destroy the great happiness of harmony. Only when their spiritual contamination is cleansed by the student's own efforts, their unhappiness dispersed, will a life of innocent happiness be experienced by good disciples to whom the master offers his heart and achieved knowledge."

SEVENTY-FOUR

"Venerable Teacher, in the practice of complete spiritual cultivation, what deities and divine beings should one connect oneself with for the purpose of energy response?"

"Kind prince," replied the master, "the universe is the body of the godhead. Most of the time we treat it as the great goddess of the feminine principle. The pure being of man and woman is the spiritual symbol as well as the reality of the angelic beings. The *T'ai Chi* circle is the spiritual emblem, and *Hu Tu* and *Lu Su* the divine diagram. The Eight Great Manifestations and sixty-four hexagrams of the *I Ching* are the revelation of the truth of universal harmony. The sun of fire and the moon of water are the spiritual symbols of masculine and feminine. Mountains are the symbols of the young male, and lakes the symbols of young females. Towers and ponds are built for the spiritual purpose of symbolizing male and female energy and for expressing and evoking specific energy responses from the mystical source. The entire practice is associated with the manifestation of the unimaginable, indescribable Universal Divine Energy. It is beyond the scope of words! Yet, with the purpose of kindling your spiritual energy in your body, the 'Universal Divine One' should be worshiped."

SEVENTY-FIVE

The master continued the dialogue, saying, "Kind prince, look at the silkworm. At first it is only a small pink spot of an egg, but when the spring warmth hatches it, the tiny worm starts to break through its shell and becomes a black grub that feeds on young, green mulberry leaves. As it grows, the black color slowly fades away and the worm becomes fat and white. When it is old enough, it stops eating and begins spitting out silk on all sides of its body to make a cocoon in order to prepare for its second transformation into a pupa. When it emerges from the cocoon as a moth, it has a distinct gender and it copulates with a moth of the opposite sex. After giving his physical essence to the female moth, the male moth dies away. The female moth conceives and brings forth eggs, but then she too dies away. This is the cycle of a silkworm's life, which is governed entirely by biological law.

"Kind prince, what do you think? From a biological point of view, how much difference is there between a human life and the life of a silkworm?"

"Venerable Teacher, through numberless years of struggling, mankind has grown in self-awareness, yet from the beginning of life, I do not see any difference between silkworms and human beings, except for those individuals who are born of Heaven."

"Kind prince, even those who are Heaven-born must obey the law of human life when they take human form. The law of human beings is basically the same as the law of silkworms."

"Venerable Teacher, I feel sad that even though people develop and grow in self-awareness, they are still bound by the biological pattern of birth, growth, procreation and death. Is it not a pity that people do not have the opportunity to learn the path of liberation from the physical bondage?"

"Kind prince, liberation from physical bondage and high spiritual freedom are not beautiful pavilions in the air. They require a process of continual transformation and evolution with the biological aspect of a human being as its foundation. It involves breaking through the cycle of life and death. It forms the hope of every individual who would attain the freedom of life. Most people's awareness is limited to the short span of their own lifetime and the superficial sphere of their daily life, as they stubbornly insist that these ordinary cycles are the final truth of life. They superstitiously cling to the hope that they will receive salvation through their religious beliefs, thus they see no need to learn the Universal Way of cultivation."

"Venerable Teacher, in future generations and in the time of confusion, will there be good men and women who have the opportunity to know the truth of a free immortal life and who will succeed in breaking through their own cycles of life and death?"

"Kind prince, in future generations, because people procreate as prolifically as the silkworm produces eggs, with little moral control or astrological awareness, there will inevitably be many disabled and sick individuals. This blind and ignorant multiplication of the population will degrade the quality of humanity. In the future there will also be collective murder, slaughter, plagues, and finally a big war with the crisis of total destruction. Because of the destructive tendency of the undeveloped world, this is what seems to be approaching."

"Venerable Teacher, what can we do for the future generations of our descendants?"

"Kind prince, the Universal Way and the eternal truth of life depend on the development of individual self-awareness, not shallow social movements for the multitudes. What is needed is the total awakening of all, so that the majority of people will know to eliminate negative influences in their lives and do what would benefit other people. Universal cultivation is individually based because it involves personal self-transformation and breaking through the individual's cycle of insatiability. Each individual is responsible for his own evolution, but true achievement comes mostly from one's virtuous fulfillment in helping and serving his fellow human.

"The teaching service is to show the way to those of great potential virtue. Surely, the teacher gives a strong positive discipline for self-cultivation, however, he cannot perform an individual's self-cultivation for him nor undergo the disciple's self-transformation. If there is no teacher, there is no way to receive the training and discipline necessary for continual cultivation. The teacher is a subtle mold in which the disciple may shape himself. If the disciple can maintain enough malleability to transform himself inwardly and outwardly, he may derive a new spirit and a new life. There is a saying that only by breaking down his resistance to the new can a disciple receive the new light.

"A teacher of universal life is an angel who resides in the world to help people. He radiates his virtue to nourish his surroundings and, if he is misunderstood by people, he does not stop extending his virtue to them. Also with his integral awareness, he cannot be enslaved by the world. In future generations the world may not become a slaughter house, if teachers of universal life are respected and their precious teaching seen as the safeguard of each generation of life."

"Venerable Teacher, I wish for all divine beings to have mercy on humankind and save them from perishing."

"Kind prince, a time of world destruction will not come in the future in which many lives are lost if those who are able to save themselves and the world practice selfless virtuous fulfillment and follow the Universal Way of life. Only the ones of immortal virtue will be able to support the world and start a better one."

"Human beings are descendants of divine origin, but they have degraded themselves generation after generation until, at last, all self-awareness has been lost. In their blindness, they could easily destroy themselves and the world they live in. In the human world this has happened on a small scale many times before, particularly at the climax of some human cultures. But a new world has always been re-created by virtuous beings. These events have been known to the highly developed ones for a long time. Kind prince, virtuous people are concerned with the future of all lives. Beside the positive, virtuous efforts to awaken their fellow man to trust in the divine subtle law which manifests itself in *T'ai Chi*, there is always the remedy of the extreme offsetting itself by over expansion."

SEVENTY-SIX

The master continued, "Kind prince, all who follow the guidance in this scripture will attain the correct awareness of the integral, universal life of truth. Their minds will become calm and they will develop subtle potency. They will extend their virtue unconditionally to all of their fellow beings. When integral virtue prevails in the world, neither the potencies of the spirits of physical nature nor the rulers of the world can do any harm. When the potencies of the spirits of physical nature and the rulers of the world merge into one united whole, all virtuous energy will unite and benefit all life."

"Venerable Teacher," said the prince, "allow me to make my vow before my only teacher, the one of universal, integral virtue. I vow to embrace the integral Oneness and ignore all divergence. As an expression of the divine nature of my life, I vow to extend integral, universal virtue to the world without putting personal consideration first."

"Kind prince, one who realizes his virtuous responsibility to quietly offer himself to others without expecting a reward or honor can be entrusted with the life of the entire world. Indeed, he becomes the savior of the world."

SEVENTY-SEVEN

"Venerable Teacher, should this scripture be called 'The Thorough Emancipation of the Mind,' although in truth there is no mind to emancipate, or should it be called 'The Integration of Universal Mind?' Will the general public in the future time of confusion be able to benefit from such high instruction?   Will it even be powerful enough to lead sensitive individuals out of darkness?"

"Kind prince," asked the master, "will the people of the future be less intelligent?"

"Venerable Teacher," replied the prince, "I think people of the future will be more intelligent, so I do not understand why there will be more trouble in the future. Although life will be more abundant, people will be more unhappy. Why is this so?"

"Wise prince," replied the master, "it will be from the misuse and partial development of intelligence that a time of confusion will arise and grow progressively worse. People will lose their appreciation for a healthy natural life of plainness after being attracted to and entrapped by all kinds of accumulated bad habits. Slavery will pervade human life and all human relationships under different names and reasons. If one is not the slave of social undevelopment, he will be the slave of all kinds of emotional entrapment; if not the slave of his desires, then the slave of his ego. The forms of slavery are many. Most people become slaves to natural demands, fashionable luxuries, social power, artificial religion or ideology, destiny, and most of all, psychological excuses. All kinds of unnecessary conflict will be brought about, aggravating turmoil and creating unprecedented calamity on a large scale.

"Kind prince, the Universal Way will be available at all times and places for the problems of individuals and the world. There will be great people who awaken during the era of great confusion and darkness. Through a vast social renaissance, the awakening of the universal divine nature within people will be reached. Its true foundation rests on the people who will achieve themselves through individual emancipation and self-cultivation.

"To achieved individuals, it is true that there is no mind to be emancipated, and neither is there any mind to be enslaved, but, in general, people create a variety of complicated situations and become stuck in their concepts and false images. They remain unaware of the situation on the large scale by being stuck and trying to convince others to follow what they think is right. Thus, confusion is added to confusion and slaves follow other slaves in terrible darkness.

"Kind prince, what do you think? Will a person become very different as an individual after being emancipated from all kinds of slavery?"

"Venerable Teacher, before being emancipated from all kinds of slavery, one lives like a blind man who continually falls into the mud and does not complain of his blindness, but only of being in the mud. One who has emancipated himself from slavery of all kinds sees the light at all times."

"Kind prince, to an integrally achieved one, there is no more blindness and no more mud, so there is no more separation of any kind. Complete emancipation takes place only when one integrates all aspects of a natural, healthy life.

"The Universal One dissolves all shallow, sensory discrimination in order to serve the universal Oneness of integral life. The Universal One does not even strive to embrace Oneness, because to do so would establish the concepts of self and Oneness. Oneness is all embracing, and it is also non-embracing. The Universal One embraces nothing, because there is nothing to hinder him or her from extending one's true nature to embrace all things and beings. The Universal One is simply natural and truthful. To be nothing apart from one's true nature is to be all."

"Venerable Teacher, will people become so afraid of being enslaved that they will not dare to do anything at all?"

"Kind prince, a person of complete emancipation has also emancipated himself from the concept of being a slave. People who look for true mastery should realize that mastery comes from lowering oneself. They should not be afraid of being positively committed to living a virtuous life. Those who restore their true nature achieve balance, integration and harmony. They become universal beings whose virtue is complete and impartial.

"When one is completely emancipated from what he has built around himself, what is left is his pure nature. A person can then spontaneously release his pure energy in daily life, so that his very essence is connected with the entire universe. He is thus regarded as a person of truth.

"A person of truth is a living divinity. He is not only above his mind, but he can be above the laws of physical nature. He actually becomes one with all. When he moves, the universe moves. When he sleeps, the universe sleeps. This is not merely a philosophical notion; it is living truth. A person of truth is so simple that he cannot be distinguished from other people, yet he can be recognized by those who have developed to the same level."

SEVENTY-EIGHT

"Venerable Teacher," said the prince, "you have shown us the way to integralness so that those who aspire to learn it in the future will clearly be able to understand that the Universal Way is a matter of living wholly and not the religious invention of a desperate mind. It is pure universal mind itself, not a mental concept. It is the depth of the wholesome mind, not mere cleverness that reacts to external circumstance. It is pure energy, not the mirage which people mistake for spiritual achievement. It is the continuous development of life with its spirits, not the result of hypnosis. It is the plain, natural truth, not philosophical fantasy. It is invariable, universal law, not a cultural flower produced by one time and place. It is the eternal unfolding of life, not a psychological approach to quiet the troubled, wounded mind. It is total reality, not an occult practice. It is the true way of fulfillment in life.

"The Universal Way is the constant, immutable truth of the multi-universe. Any oddity, strangeness or fanaticism goes against it. Extravagant lifestyles, fancy food and raucous music spoil the serenity of the mind and dull one's subtlety; life becomes barren and one's spiritual unfolding is obstructed. The Universal Way values simplicity, plainness and virtue in speech, dress and behavior far more than that which is exciting, dazzling and fashionable. Through establishing honesty in every facet of life, one may return to the simple essence of life. Excessiveness and extremes are contrary to the Universal Integral Way and are therefore never practiced by one who follows the Way of wholeness."

"Venerable Teacher, I truly understand that the development of one's being through self-cultivation is the only correct way of life. Because a human being is so malleable, whatever one cultivates is what one becomes. If one tries to practice cultivation by following a particular religious doctrine, one becomes a slave to partiality. Worldly religion is meant to hold some people of the world, but it also creates disharmony among people on a larger scale. When one takes a single step outside the human sphere of life, all religious practices become useless because they are nothing more than hypnotic, psychological techniques for manipulating an undeveloped mind. The habitual effect of religion on the mind is a real obstacle to pure spiritual growth, and when one departs from artificial teachings and is free of any religious control, one may find that no spiritual evolution has taken place by merely following a religion. Is it not a pity that so many are manipulated by the misbelief that religion can save their souls?"

"Kind prince, if one's spiritual pursuit is partial, one's development is partial. Universal beings are completely evolved from and in the human sphere, having refined the three spheres of energy of a human being. When one cultivates oneself correctly, an internal transformation takes place. The internal metamorphosis is subtle and gradual, and is usually unobservable to those who are undeveloped. When one's energy is ripe, however, the old self is transformed just as a caterpillar is transformed into a beautiful butterfly.

"Kind prince, if one does not find the right way of refining one's physical energy to become spiritual immortal elixir and merely looks for philosophical or psychological satisfaction, he will not be able to break through his human, biological limitations and evolve to a higher state of being.

"Before a person achieves transformation from the gross sphere to the subtle spiritual realms, he may return to the dusty world many times. His life experiences may be similar or different each time, but the general rule is that if a person takes the partial events of his life either too seriously or too lightly, he spoils his opportunity.

"Once a person achieves complete transformation and sublimation, he becomes unfathomable. No ordinary means of measuring or judging can be applied to him. He is a Universal One who can come and go as anyone else, but his essence of life always exists. He can do and make good things happen but not necessarily through himself. There is nothing that he is unable to do. He extends his pure life to many bodies which appear in different places and can do many things at the same time, because, in truth, he has attained the subtle, cosmic body. He is the one who can actualize all positive virtues but keeps to the subtle source. This is not a mere philosophical notion. One will miss the truth of a Universal Being by not realizing true self-cultivation.

"A universal being can outlive any time and any generation. Mere understanding does not enable one to become a universal being, but through actual self-cultivation and direct realization, one verifies the truth and fulfills the universal truth by being it. The truth is here in the simple essence of life when one is ready to accept it, but people look for it instead in far-away shadows."

SEVENTY-NINE

"Venerable Teacher, in the future time of confusion, will the one who studies and practices this scripture be able to gain the integral vision of the universal subtle truth?"

"Kind prince, the one who studies and practices this scripture will attain the insight to see through to the universal truth."

"Venerable Teacher, will those people of the future who study and practice this scripture acquire the subtle light of wisdom?"

"Kind prince, they will acquire the subtle light that illuminates all time and space."

"Venerable Teacher, will those who study and practice this scripture in the future acquire the mightiest sword of superior mind?"

"Kind prince, those who study and practice this scripture will obtain the sharp sword of clarity that thrusts through all entanglements and obstruction."

"Venerable Teacher, will those who study and practice this scripture in the future obtain the mystical pearl of full development?"

"Kind prince, they will grow a mystical pearl of full development which can expand to envelop the entire universe and can also gather itself into an invisible seed of smallness."

"Venerable Teacher, will those who study and practice this scripture in the future achieve the undaunted moral courage and undestroyable power of Universal Nature?"

"Kind prince, they shall achieve the undaunted moral courage and undestroyable power of Universal Nature.

"What do you think, kind prince. Can one describe the integral vision of the universal subtle truth?"

"No, Venerable Teacher, the integral vision of the universal subtle truth cannot be described, however, one could say that when the opening of a fountain is blocked with sand, the fountain cannot flow."

"Kind prince, what is the sand that blocks the fountain's flow?"

"Venerable Teacher, it is irrational, dualistic vision which blocks the fountain of universal mindedness."

"Kind prince, does the subtle light of wisdom have a specific shape?"

"Venerable Teacher, the subtle light of wisdom is without shape."

"Kind prince, does the mighty sword of clarity have a specific form?"

"No, Venerable Teacher, the mighty sword of clarity is without any form."

"Kind prince, what does the mystical pearl of full development look like?"

"Venerable Teacher, it looks like nothing."

"Kind prince, what do you think? Can the undestroyable Universal Nature be measured?"

"No, Venerable Teacher, the undestroyable Universal Nature is immeasurable. It is absolutely powerful, however."

"Kind prince, those who study and practice the truth of this scripture in future generations will be blessed. By following its integral guidance with sincerity they will gain the most mysterious power. They will become indestructible and will rise above all difficulty and calamity.

"Kind prince, what do you think? Did I obtain any secret knowledge from my master?"

"Venerable Teacher, I truly believe that you received boundless treasures from past masters."

"Kind prince, do you now have the integral vision of the universal subtle truth?"

"Yes, Venerable Teacher, I have attained the integral vision of the universal subtle truth through your precious guidance."

"Kind prince, do you now have the mighty sword of wisdom and clarity of superior mind?"

"Yes, Venerable Teacher, I have acquired both through your precious training."

"Kind prince, have you restored the integral nature of indestructibility?"

"Yes, Venerable Teacher, I have restored the integral nature of indestructibility through practicing universal mindedness and universal heartedness."

"Kind prince, are these treasures visible?"

"Venerable Teacher, they are invisible."

"Kind prince, can one assign a name to the all-encompassing integralness?"

"No, Venerable Teacher, although it is referred to as the Way, the integralness of universal beingness is unnameable."

"Kind prince, does the Way exist as something apart from one's own being?"

"No, Venerable Teacher, the Way is not something separate or external to one's own being. However, some human beings who are partially developed spiritually or intellectually will perceive it as such."

"Kind prince, what then is the Way?"

"Venerable Teacher, I cannot respond in words, I can only embrace it in wholeness."

"Kind prince, do not embrace the Way. Be the Way."

EIGHTY

"Venerable Teacher, should one live in seclusion and cultivate oneself in order to transcend all worldly troubles and pain or should one courageously take on the troubles and pain of worldly experiences as important elements in attaining enlightenment and integral virtue?"

"Kind prince, if one does not become thoroughly enlightened in order to reach unshakable integralness, one can face neither the solitude of seclusion nor the pressure of living in the world. Only those who are fully enlightened are able to use one hand to assist the other. Enlightenment is the means, virtue is the end. One who is truly wise is virtuous.

"Kind prince, it is not a question of whether one should live in seclusion or in the world. The question is will one really achieve complete enlightenment and spiritual freedom, or will one become only partially enlightened? If one achieves only partial enlightenment, he may become clever, sharp tongued and so overly sensitive that he is unable to bear the task of living in the practical world. He may insist on isolating himself to enjoy his so-called spiritual pleasures alone, or he may rush to impart his own teachings to the world. In any of these instances, the person deviates from the Way."

"Venerable Teacher, if all of these alternatives are but a deviation, what is the correct course to take?"

"Kind prince, a great vessel takes a long time to shape. An individual's enlightenment is arrived at through long and tedious cultivation. One who desires to reach the climax of his cultivation too soon and strives to publicize himself prematurely may become a false model of virtue and sacrifice the truth or even his own life through ignorance. He may lose himself and mislead others without ever having a chance to correct his wrongdoing if he were to die young. In the future the streets will be full of self-proclaimed, but half-enlightened, teachers who will bring about much confusion."

"Venerable Teacher, the human world seems like a big ship in need of someone to steer it. If there is no one at the helm, it could drift aimlessly into dangerous waters and imperil the lives of all its passengers. There must be someone who is willing to shoulder the responsibility of navigating the vessel of the world. In the future time of confusion, will there be people who are virtuous enough to keep the world headed in a positive direction on its voyage?"

"Kind prince, a person of the universal subtle truth is not ambitious to be a leader unless the responsibility falls to him; he will make no scheme to take it. He fulfills the task that is assigned to him and then takes no credit and holds no attachment to it. He merely offers himself to serve others. He knows that individuals are the foundation of human society, thus the way to guide the world is to correctly guide each person who comes to him. This work does not merely skim the surface of the social problem, but goes deeply into the source. Whoever undertakes such an endeavor must prepare himself to meet the following qualifications.

"One must deeply plant and firmly root one's spirit in the universal subtle truth. One must be truly virtuous and sincere. At a practical level one must be willing to improve himself by eliminating all negative attitudes and habits. In this way one is able to build a stable, broad, receptive and creative personality. Only then may one plunge into the ocean of bountiful spiritual knowledge and training to become a Mentor of the Universal Way."

"Kind prince, true Mentors are the embodiment of heavenly energy. They are the direct expression of the universal subtle truth. They must have attained spiritual maturity through true life experience in the world. Then they can become the spiritual light to those in darkness. To be with them is to experience the living truth. Their minds are as deep and all-encompassing as the Universal Truth. By breaking through the mystery of life and death and the dream-like quality of their own mental faculty they have fully developed and integrated all aspects of their being, and their personal nature is one with the Universal Truth. Their speech and behavior are the manifestation of their own spiritual attainment, responding to the different personalities and environments they encounter. Their lives are an expression of wisdom and pure law. They are the revelation of the mystery of the great universal triad: Heaven, Earth and Man. Their smiles radiate light, wisdom and bliss. They teach others selflessly, not out of any desire for self-aggrandizement. They are the true father and mother, true brother and sister, and true friend of their disciples. Their grace always illuminates the dark corners of the disciples' minds. They share their divine energy with their disciples and are always aware of their problems. They dissolve their disciples' pain in the ocean of their compassion. The sadness, imperfection and false personalities of the disciples vanish before their eyes and they see only the disciples' true nature.

"Because they know the traps and obstacles of life, they can guide their disciples out of troubled waters. The trials they give their disciples are a process of strengthening and building. They sometimes scold their disciples in an attempt to awaken them; if a disciple misunderstands this, loses faith, and gives up everything, it means he has fallen from the spiritual path and failed himself. If a disciple is foolish enough to rely on his own cleverness, he will endlessly go around and around in the false illusion of his own ego.

"True masters can awaken the disciples' divine energy and lead them to enlightenment. They can direct the stream of their disciples' lives toward the infinite ocean of Universal Truth. A good disciple humbly and gratefully accepts the master so that he or she can proceed directly on the true path of Universal Truth. With love, gratitude and sincerity, the disciple should be willing to dedicate his entire being to the master and his teaching, to respectfully accept the instructions of the master and faithfully follow, serve and obey the master. If a disciple remains single-purposed and unwavering in his self-cultivation, he will surely attain self-mastery and become qualified to guide others to do the same."

EIGHTY-ONE

As the old master was about to conclude his dialogue, he inquired of the prince and all his disciples, "Kind prince and all of my beloved friends, I have talked a lot. Did I really say anything since you have been with me? My dear disciples, since I started my journey to the West I have not said one thing. The subtle truth cannot be concluded in words. What all of you have listened to is the eternal breath of the Universal Truth which has been emanating through me and all of you. The subtle voice of the universal origin has been speaking since the beginning of the universe. To those whose energy can respond to it, this sound is very distinct. To those whose energy cannot respond to it, the sound is muffled and obscure. The subtle melody of universal life is eternal and constant, yet only those who are in consonance with it can perceive it.

"Kind prince, listen only to one who speaks with life. Obey that law which is so subtle it cannot be written. Follow only the one who does not show himself. Worship the unformed, embrace the unnamed and unite yourself with what is not entrapped by any form that existed before Heaven, Earth or Man. Respect the one who makes no demands. Say what cannot be said in words. Have intercourse with the subtle. Offer unconditional love to all life and trust the invariable, positive nature of the universe.

"My beloved disciples, a universal integral being never comes and goes. The voice of the Universal One will always be with you! Always listen for the non-verbal voice and you will reach the Divine Origin. When all words are exhausted, the truth appears.

"Be happy and content with your universal nature, for this is where we can meet and embrace each other and be together eternally. Never be bewildered by any transitory phenomena. Steadfastly keep pace with the subtle, eternal, divine energy within and without."

The master finished his dialogue, and the audience, both beings and non-beings, greatly rejoiced at having had the opportunity to learn the Universal Way. They sincerely accepted and cherished the teaching and maintained it as the only true guidance in their lives. They practiced their virtue and refined themselves while living in the world. A healthy, natural life was their standard of living. Their work was an expression of their virtue and a reward for their creative minds and hands. They maintained balance and harmony as the essential principles of their lives. They followed the integral truth of the universe and were not inclined to follow any partial doctrine. They chose the fellowship of integral truth as the unified expression of their spiritual vantage point.

Periodic retreat from society was their renaissance, yet they did not use their retreat as an excuse for inertia or as an escape from their spiritual obligation to awaken and purify the world. They realized that a normal, balanced life is much more important than full-time retreat. They lived and worked in the world without being affected by it. They maintained themselves as contemplative hermits without the need to withdraw from the world and become self-enclosed. They quietly continued the divine spiritual mission by making the natural, spiritual, traditional education available to all people in any generation; following the describable to cultivate the indescribable, performing that which can be spoken of in order to arrive at that which cannot be spoken of. Many of them accomplished their worldly mission and inner evolution, and spiritually ascended to the divine realms in broad daylight with their physical lives. Those indestructible universal souls, whether returning to the physical world again as human beings or enjoying the subtle realm eternally, are the true essence of universal life. It is they who continue to inspire the precious truths of the universe in their human disciples in order to preserve the sacred teaching of the Universal Way as the true guidance for all natural lives.

Resources

Tao of Wellness Health Center

1131 Wilshire Boulevard, Suite 300
Santa Monica, CA 90401
310-917-2200
www.taoofwellness.com

The Tao of Wellness Health Center is the integral way to total well-being and a long life. Each patient is seen as an individual whose health is immediately affected by his or her lifestyle including diet, habits, emotions, attitude, and environment. The center, co-founded by Drs. Daoshing and Maoshing Ni, focuses on acupuncture and Chinese herbs for complete health, longevity, and fertility.

Tao of Wellness Herbs and Books

13315 W. Washington Boulevard, Suite 200
Los Angeles, CA 90066
800-772-0222; 310-302-1207
www.taostar.com
taostar@taostar.com

Nourishing Chinese herbal products from the 38th-generation Ni Family Healing tradition. Books on Taoist teachings to nurture the spirit and to provide tools for positive living. Tai Chi and qigong on DVD and video; guided meditation on CD and audio tapes. Please contact us for a free catalog.

Yo San University of Traditional Chinese Medicine

13315 W. Washington Boulevard, 2nd floor
Los Angeles, CA 90066
877.967.2648; 310.577.3000
www.yosan.edu

One of the finest and most academically rigorous Traditional Chinese Medical schools in the United States, Yo San University offers a fully accredited Master's degree program in acupuncture, herbology, *tui na* body work, and *chi* movement arts. In this program, students explore their spiritual growth as an integral part of learning the healing arts.

Chi Health Institute
PO Box 2035
Santa Monica, California 90406-2035
310-577-3031
www.taostar.com

The *Chi* Health Institute (CHI) offers professional education and certification in the Ni family *chi* movement arts including *t'ai chi*, *qi gong*, and Taoist meditation.

Integral Way Society
PO Box 1530
Santa Monica, CA 90406-1530
www.taostar.com

Learn about classical Taoist teachings transmitted by the Ni family through books, mentoring, and retreats organized by the Integral Way Society. The IWS assists people in achieving physical, mental, and spiritual health by nurturing self-respect and by offering methods of self-improvement based on the principles in the classic works of the *I Ching* and Lao Tzu's *Tao Teh Ching*.

Chinese Nutrition: Distance Learning Course
www.taostar.com

Apply the classic concepts and power of Traditional Chinese Medicine to the selection of daily foods. Basic understanding and practical application of nutrition theories including food energetics, survey of Zang-Fu syndromes, and patient consultation. Up to 45 hours of CEU credit available.

College of Tao: Distance Learning Course
PO Box 1222
El Prado, NM 87529
www.taostar.com

The College of Tao offers an introduction to spiritual self-development through an internet study program that is constructed to support students who have read one or more books on the Integral Way of Life. Designed for those who want to deepen their understanding and experience of the Integral Way, students learn to apply its principles to their daily lives.

Infinichi Institute International

PO Box 26712
San Jose, CA 95159-6712
408-295-5911
www.taostar.com

Professional training in *chi* healing leading to certification as an InfiniChi Practitioner. The program is designed to develop your energetic healing abilities utilizing the Ni family books and texts that relate to Traditional Chinese Medicine, *qi gong*, Chinese bodywork, and natural spirituality. It features a progressive, systematic program that nurtures understanding, facilitates skill development, and promotes self-growth.

Acupuncture.com

www.acupuncture.com

Acupuncture.com is the gateway to Chinese medicine, health, and wellness. From this site you can purchase Tao of Wellness herbal products and a large selection of patent herbs as well as acupuncture books and products.

Index